Original China
Stoneware

Oldest English Silver
1670-71

Silver Tea-Kettle
c 1712

Ast

Rockingham

Sheffield Plate

Barge teapot
c 1890

Old Hall Stainless Steel

Wedgwood-Contemporary

Tea and Coffee

Tea caddy made by Joseph Bramah as a boy in Yorkshire, in 1766, and now in the possession of the author. It is $4\frac{1}{2}$ in. high with two compartments for green and black tea. The decoration is paper filigree, a popular technique of the time.

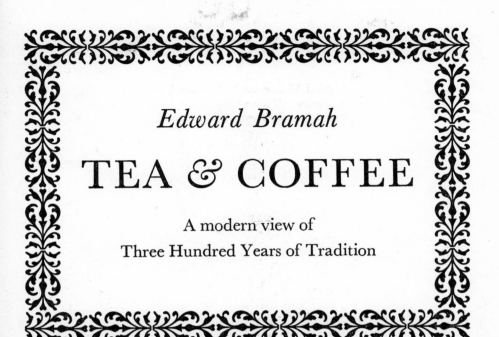

Edward Bramah

TEA & COFFEE

A modern view of
Three Hundred Years of Tradition

HUTCHINSON OF LONDON

HUTCHINSON & CO (*Publishers*) LTD
3 Fitzroy Square, London W1

London Melbourne Sydney Auckland
Wellington Johannesburg Cape Town
and agencies throughout the world

First published 1972

*This book has been set in Baskerville type, printed in Great Britain
on cartridge paper by Anchor Press, and
bound by Wm. Brendon, both of Tiptree, Essex*

ISBN 0 09 108950 6

Contents

Acknowledgements

Much of the material for this book is the result of my having had the good fortune to work in different sections of the tea and coffee trades, and not least from being able to learn my job from friendly superiors and colleagues. In particular I must mention the manager of Thornwood Estate, R. R. A. Bishop; David Theobald of the Tea Buying Department at J. Lyons and Co. Ltd., and W. Robert Forder, who is now adviser to the Ethiopian Coffee Board.

I am also indebted to the late C. J. P. Simpson of C. J. Valentine Ltd., Nairobi, and J. A. M. Meston of Gow Wilson & Co. Ltd., London for the encouragement they have given me during the early part of my career.

Throughout the time I have been writing this book, I have had much ungrudging help from Mr. R. Dennis of the Ceylon Tea Centre, which possesses a unique collection of historical tea photographs, and for the excellent photographs of tea production in Malawi I must acknowledge the co-operation of the Ministry of Trade and Industry, Blantyre and Mr. W. D. Simfukwe of the High Commissioner's Office in London.

I am indebted to Mr. O. A. Makule, Chairman of the Tanganyika Coffee Board, Moshi, Tanzania, for his assistance in updating my knowledge of Tanganyika coffees and for supplying photographs. Further help with photographs was also given by the Director of Information Services, the Ministry of Information and Tourism, Dar es Salaam. In the chapter on coffee in East Africa I have also used some magnificent photographs supplied by Mr. Grupfeldt of Interpret, Hamburg, to whom I was introduced by Mr. H. G. Davis, Overseas Representative of the Kenya Coffee Industry.

For the checking of certain technical points regarding tea chemistry and customs procedure I am most grateful to Dr. Amphlett Williams, Public Analyst to the Port of London Health Authority, with whom I shared some experience concerning tea in 1960.

Throughout the book I have referred constantly for information to William H. Ukers' standard works *All About Tea* and *All About*

Coffee, and for allowing me to use several photographs I must thank the *Tea and Coffee Trade Journal,* New York. During the writing of the tea- and coffee-brewing chapter I was assisted by G. B. L. Wilson, Deputy Keeper of the Science Museum, South Kensington, who has a most comprehensive knowledge of domestic appliances, and whose time was most freely given.

Without the co-operation of G. E. R. Pearl, Managing Director of *Vending Times,* it would have been virtually impossible to have assembled the material for the vending chapter and I thank him sincerely for the loan of his collection of back numbers of *Vending and Modern Catering* which he first published in 1958. I was also assisted by W. E. D. Skinner, Chief Executive of the Automatic Vending Association of Britain.

In the last chapter, which I have tried to make as accurate and up-to-date as possible, I am indebted to J. A. Patterson of Wood-house, Drake & Carey Ltd., and to Bickford of The London Produce Clearing House Ltd., for his information about the working of the Coffee Terminal Market. My researches on tea were greatly facilitated by the co-operation of the staff of R. S. Hawkins, Editor of the Tea and Rubber Mail section of the *Investors Guardian.*

Finally, I cannot end these acknowledgements without expressing appreciation to my wife who has spent many hours typing and reading through the manuscript and without whose help this book would never have been written.

Preface

Tea and coffee are exotic and exciting tropical crops, pleasant to grow and unendingly fascinating to deal in. The men who first went out to India and Ceylon and Africa to clear the jungle and open up new areas for great plantations had the same pioneering spirit and faced similar dangers as the gold prospectors of Australia or the Voortrekkers of South Africa. The quarter-pound packets of tea and half-pound tins of coffee which appear with unfailing reliability on the grocers' shelves are the result of hundreds of years of patient horticulture and constant improvements in manufacturing methods. They are also there because of the integrity and vast knowledge of the handful of men with trained palates and years of experience who make up the City of London tea and coffee trade and perform the vital task of getting the chests of tea and bags of green beans from the producers to the public.

Banking is business, oil is industry, tea and coffee are trade, but the tea trade in particular has always had a special aristocratic position in the world of buying and selling. Galsworthy's Forsytes founded a large part of their family fortune on tea. Old Jolyon did so well out of China tea in Mincing Lane that he maintained a large house in Stanhope Gate, Park Lane, and died leaving £145,000. No broker today could amass the modern equivalent of such a fortune, even if he cornered the whole of the tea market, but the small band of brokers and the even smaller number of major tea companies between them account for more than 500 million lb. of tea a year worth £100 million sterling. Coffee is not yet so important, but imports are rising fast and the London Terminal Market not only deals in coffee consumed in this country but also transacts deals in coffee destined for other countries.

These specialised tea and coffee worlds are not easy to get into. They are for the most part shrinking and careers in them never seem nowadays to appear on the careers masters' lists. The tea planter's job is straightforward enough, but the plantations are in parts of the world which are now almost closed to Englishmen. I was lucky twenty years ago to find an opening in a country which had not yet been granted independence.

After I completed my National Service in the Navy in 1950 I had intended to go into a career in banking, preferably overseas, but a day or two before my interview in London I met a tea planter home on leave from Africa who changed my mind and inspired in me an enthusiasm for tea and tropical agriculture which I have never lost. My first attempt at getting a job with a producing company was a failure. They wanted a young man with a degree from an agricultural college, but this refusal only made me more determined. On the morning that I got the letter turning me down, I caught a train to London and went to Nyasaland House and made a list of all the companies growing tea there, intending to work my way through their London head offices. By the afternoon I had managed to get an interview with Rosehaugh Tea and Rubber Estates and in three weeks I was on my way to Mlanje, Nyasaland. A few years later I started a career in coffee in almost the same way, although it is rare for anyone working in tea ever to leave it for another crop.

In my twenty years in tea and coffee there have been many occasions when I have needed information on my two subjects and I have always been surprised that apart from detailed manuals for planters there are so few books about them. There are, it is true, two encyclopaedic tomes edited by William Ukers which were written in the 1920's and 1930's and contained in their day practically everything then known about tea and coffee, but they are very expensive and long out of print and all available copies have permanent homes in the offices of the tea trade. The general public would probably find them dull and unenlightening and for this reason I decided to attempt to fill the gap myself.

Immediately the difficulty arose as to how to write a book about both tea and coffee, which are vastly different in history and production although firmly linked commercially and domestically. I could have written two books of carefully impersonal accounts of cultivation, manufacture and social history, but these would have omitted what I most wanted to convey, the sheer fascination of making a working life in tea and coffee. Since the last twenty years have brought me into contact with every aspect of both commodities from their cultivation to the final moment when they are served in a cup, I decided that I would present my information in the order in which I discovered it myself, and I hope that although this may seem at first glance a chaotic method of approach, it does result in a reasonably logical form of presentation. I have tried, in fact, not just to describe the history of a leaf and a bean, but to illuminate two small worlds.

Many of the photographs in this book are familiar classics, but I feel they are worth reproducing. The illustrations of tea and coffee manufacture are from African countries, not only because of my personal connection with that continent, but also because Africa is one of the fastest developing parts of the world in tea and coffee production and possesses some of the most modern methods of cultivation and manufacture.

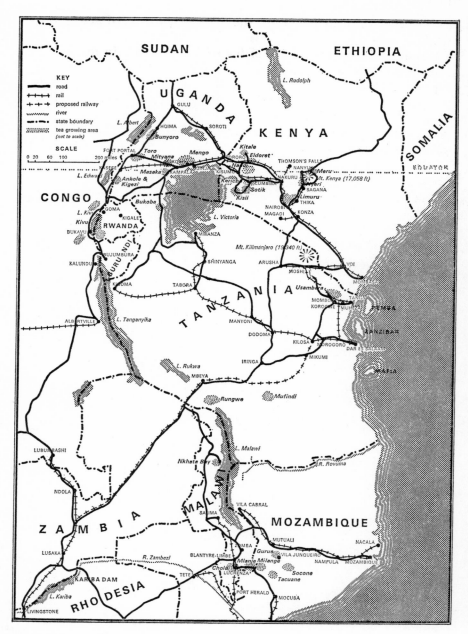

The tea estates of East Africa

I

Tea Country

The camellia is an evergreen plant from sub-tropical and tropical Asia. The species most familiar in this country is the camellia japonica or florist's camellia with its luscious red, pink or white flowers and shiny, vividly green leaves, but it has two cousins, not so superficially attractive, but far more commercially important. These are camellia sinensis and camellia assamica, known to the non-botanical world as tea.

Camellia sinensis, or Chinese camellia, has been grown in China for hundreds, perhaps thousands, of years, but its origins are not in the black-tea provinces of Fukien and Kwangtung, or in the green-tea provinces of Anhwei and Chekiang. The wild plant from which cultivated tea must have developed has never been found in southern China. It originated, with wild India tea, in that remote part of South-East Asia where the Yangtze runs south out of the Tibetan Highlands and turns east near the source of the Brahmaputra and the Irrawaddy. Even now there is some doubt whether camellia sinensis and camellia assamica are separate sub-species or whether they are both descended from some common ancestor and have developed in their different ways to east and west, separated by the watershed of the Patkai Highlands of Burma.

When commercial tea-growing was introduced into north-east India the native plant was ignored and it was the China variety which was tried first, but it did not thrive. Outside China and Japan virtually all the tea in the world is developed from the Indian tea which was growing wild in the Brahmaputra Valley, or sometimes in rigorous climates, a hybrid of Indian and China strains.

Tea is grown over a wide range of latitudes from Georgia in South Russia in the north down to Rhodesia and South Africa and Santos in Brazil in the south. The critical requirement is rainfall. Tea does not object to a cool dry season provided the plant is a suitable type, but there must be sufficient rain in the hot season. A light, sandy loam with plenty of nitrogen to encourage leaf growth is ideal, but many types of soil will support tea, with the proviso that, in common with other species of camellia, tea dislikes lime.

Since tea is such an obligingly easy plant to grow, it is perhaps surprising that it is extremely difficult to get a good-quality tea from it. The reason is that the tea plant is like the vine. Soil, aspect, rainfall, elevation, manufacture all affect it in so many subtle ways that planting tea in a new area, evolving a suitable strain of plant, establishing it and creating the conditions for growth and manufacture which will make the tea earn a good price on the London tea market, are often the work of a generation.

In 1950, when I first decided that I wanted to plant tea, the Indian and Ceylon plantations had long-established reputations, but the old Empire was no longer a place of unlimited opportunity for a twenty-year-old Englishman. India in 1950 was still in the throes of partition troubles and was not regarded as an ideal country to start a new career in. Ceylon, newly independent, was not much better, but Africa was another matter. Malawi was still Nyasaland, Zambia was still Northern Rhodesia, Ghana was still the Gold Coast; even South Africa was still represented at the Commonwealth Conference. And the Central African Highlands had just started to make an impact on the world tea market. One of the producing companies had a vacancy for an assistant in Nyasaland, and as soon as my father had signed my contract and I could be vaccinated against smallpox and inoculated against yellow fever and typhoid I left England to start my career in tea.

The head field assistant for Rosehaugh (Nyasaland)'s Thornwood and Mimosa estates was a Scotsman and he greeted me at the air booking office at Blantyre rather as a petty officer greets a new seaman joining his ship. His smile was genuine, but I sensed that he was as apprehensive about me as I was about him. The European staff of a tea plantation usually numbered about five and a newcomer who was a misfit could be a disaster. My luggage was packed into the back of an open truck and we set off for the estate, forty-five miles away in Mlanje, on the southernmost border of Nyasaland, adjoining the Portuguese East African territory of Mozambique. The newly tarmacked road led to the flourishing tea-growing district of Cholo. This was my first sight of tea bushes. They were growing in terraces on either side of the road between trees specially planted to shade them from the sun. From Cholo to Mlanje the road was the usual unsurfaced track familiar all over Central Africa. In the distance I saw the tall factories in which the tea was processed.

Many of the estates comprised 3,000 acres with as much as a 1,000 acres under tea. They had intriguing and euphonious names: Glenorchy, Chitakali, El Dorado and Mini Mini, and above them

the great Mlanje Mountain rose almost sheer for 7,000 feet. Through
broken cloud the rays of the setting sun fell upon waterfalls and
rugged gorges, giving magnificent contrasts in light and shade. I
was looking at one of the great views of Africa. The year before,
Laurens van der Post had come to Mlanje and explored it fairly
extensively, and he gives a most vivid description of it in his book
Venture to the Interior. Although the modern tea factories were evidence
of twentieth-century progress, this corner of Africa was still very
remote. Tourists usually made for the lake resorts on Lake Nyasa
and left Mlanje alone.

In the old days of African exploration mining prospectors would
trek north from South Africa across the Zambezi and the Limpopo
rivers through Matabeleland and Mashonaland and perhaps reach
Nyasaland, tucked away in a fold of Portuguese East Africa. But
their journey was wasted. There was no copper, there were certainly
no King Solomon's Mines, and, as I found when I tried to find out
something about the area, there was still almost no information. Quite
early on a single-track railway was built from Beira on the coast
of Mozambique to Blantyre and Salisbury, Rhodesia, but this
meant that the only practical access was still from the south, and
it remained so until the pre-war hey-day of the Empire flying
boats, which could land on Lake Nyasa and also Lake Victoria
and Lake Tanganyika, opening up what had truly been Darkest
Africa.

We went direct to the head field assistant's bungalow on the
Mimosa garden where I was to stay for a few nights, but on that
first evening I learned little about my new life. While we sat drinking
coffee on the verandah, known in Nyasaland as a kondi, a tropical
storm developed, illuminating Mlanje with forked lightning. Tor-
rential rain began to beat down on the tin roof. The claps of thunder
were so deafening that conversation became impossible and there
was nothing else to do but retire to bed.

Next morning at five a houseboy wakened me with a pot of tea
and the message that Bwana Forrest had gone to work and would be
back for breakfast at eight. Dressed in an open-necked shirt and
shorts, I went out to explore my new surroundings. It seemed that
the bungalow was an island in a sea of tea bushes, and from a nearby
hill I could hear African voices and the noise of furious activity.
Jungle was being cleared in readiness for new plantings, and esti-
mating the hill to be about half a mile away, I set out to walk there.
Although the voices became clearer, the distance did not seem to
lessen, the deception being due to the crystal-clear air. The sun,
even at such an early hour, was hot on my forearms, and I had

forgotten that I should be wearing a hat.* Several hundred Africans were at work, and I realized that one of my first tasks would be to learn their language. They belonged to the Nyanja tribe, a most gentle and unwarlike people, not at all like the Zulus and the Matabele to the south and west of them. They had suffered a lot from the raids of Arab slave traders in the past, but at the turn of the century the British took over Nyasaland as a protectorate and since then the Nyanjas and the Nyasas to the north had been happy and peaceful for fifty years.

Over breakfast, which in George Forrest's well-run Scottish household always began with porridge, I learned how the garden side of an estate labour force is divided to do the various tasks through the year. In Nyasaland the weight of leaf is plucked during the rains, between October and May, when the hot sun and rain produce prolific growth on the bushes.

The first growths of the season, known as new season tippings, are plucked to allow further growths, and these, known as flushes, are plucked every seven to fourteen days. Pluckings are made in this way for six months, and are known as new season's tippings, first flush, second flush, quality, rains, autumnal and end-of-season teas. Mlanje's autumn is at the same time of the year as the English spring. During the season almost the entire labour force of several hundred is engaged in gathering the leaf, and a lot of workers come from over the Mozambique border, but in the off-season there are many other tasks to be performed, such as pruning, weeding, taking out old bushes, attending to nurseries, building dams, roads and so forth†

It is usual for the European field assistants to travel around the estates on motor-bikes. In some parts of the world they ride horses, but in Central Africa this is not possible because of tsetse fly. After breakfast I rode pillion behind George Forrest to the manager's office, calling on the way at the factory. We passed new clearings planted on high ground, and from here I could see Thornwood Estate, and behind it the eastern end of Mlanje, rising to its long flat top, known as Menene, where it is said the natives used to lay offerings to their gods. Occasionally George stopped to speak in Nyanja to an African overseer, known as a capitoe, and would give working instructions or ask for reports. He told me that the

* This was the planter's hat with the stitched brim which was becoming the established headgear for the tropics. The older generation, including the manager of Thornwood Estate, still wore the solar topee.
† The monsoon, which drenches the Indian tea plantations at the end of summer, reaches Central Africa in April, but since it comes over Mozambique first, it brings no rain.

Tea bushes growing between shade trees on the Mandimwe Estate in the Cholo district of Malawi.

African tea pluckers working on an estate at the foot of Mount Mlanje on the border of Malawi and Mozambique.

Tea factory on Pwazi Estate at the foot of Mount Mlanje, Malawi.

Two leaves and a bud. Expert pluckers at work in the Mlanje district of Malawi.

Tea assistant inspecting a basketful of leaves on its way to the factory for processing, Malawi.

Weighing the baskets of green leaf brought in by the pluckers, Malawi.

The author as a
young field assistant
on Thornwood
Estate, Malawi.

The author's bunga-
low.

Thornwood Estate
factory.

Modern withering troughs on a tea estate in Africa. This is the first stage of tea manufacture.

The withered green leaf being fed into the rolling machines for the second stage of orthodox tea manufacture.

Two machines which can either supplement or replace orthodox tea rollers. *Above*, McKercher's 'C.T.C.' machine which crushes, tears and curls the leaf; *Below*, McTear's Rotorvane, a continuous process machine, developed at Tocklai Research Station in Assam, used most extensively on the new African estates.

Above, Green leaf being spread on a table to oxidize. This stage is usually called fermentation, and as it progresses, the leaf changes colour from green to dark copper.

Left, Green leaf being taken from the rolling machine. Tea may need to be rolled more than once.

previous night's rain, some six inches of it, had washed away part of an estate road.

At the office the manager, Mr. Bishop, told me that he and his family were going home on leave and he wished me to learn the procedure for tea-processing, as the supervision of the factory would be my responsibility while he was away. He gave me a good many notes and explained in detail how tea is made and I spent the rest of the week settling down, becoming acclimatized and getting used to the layout of the estate. For the next few days I went nowhere without Mr. Bishop's precious notes and studied the individual stages of rolling, fermenting, firing and grading.

After withering, the leaf is crushed by rolling, so that the juices are freed, and under the influence of an oxidizing agent reacts chemically to form a soluble liquid which is dried on the crushed leaf, where it remains until it is freed by boiling water.

It is often said that manufacture starts in the field, and this is true; the right leaves must be plucked, all extraneous matter removed and transport to the factory carried out quickly without damage to the leaf, for if it is damaged this cannot be remedied during processing. The normal method is to pluck two leaves and a bud, but if, in addition, the coarser leaves are plucked from lower down the stem, the quantity naturally increases with a consequently greater proportion of lower-quality grades. Depending on world supplies and market trends, producers have to decide whether to concentrate on quality or quantity.

Two or three times a day the pluckers bring their baskets to a roadside collection point for the leaf to be weighed. In addition to a basic wage they receive a bonus payment on the weight of leaf gathered, and, depending on the quality of leaf plucked and the lushness of the growth, a skilled plucker may gather between 30 lb. and 60 lb. of green leaf in a day, which will yield roughly a quarter of its weight in made tea; one bush can produce enough green leaf for up to 5 oz. of made tea per year.

At that time the withering stage was carried out by spreading the green leaf on specially prepared racks, made of tightly drawn hessian or wire mesh, and allowing it to wither for from eight to twenty-four hours, during which time the leaf lost moisture and became flaccid, ready for the next process of rolling. Later, a tunnel-and-drum system was tried, but nowadays this has been superseded everywhere in the tea-producing countries by trough withering.

For what is known as the orthodox method of manufacture, the leaf is first sufficiently withered, then it is gathered in heaps of a

B

suitable weight and fed through a chute in the floor into the rollers below. These rollers are metal cylinders, open at each end, which can have a diameter up to fifty inches and hold as much as 1,000 lb. of withered leaf. The rollers, supported on large bearings, rotate in a vertical position over a table, and to assist in breaking and twisting the leaf inside the roller, a lid or pressure cap is often applied. The leaf leaves the roller in warm, sticky, twisted lumps and these are fed into coarse sieves to be cooled and broken up. The sieves are known as roll-breakers and have a shaking and sifting action. The fine, tender leaves, known as 'first quality', come through the sieve at the first roll-breaking and are removed. The remaining leaf is re-rolled and passed over the roll-breaker as many times as may be necessary to produce second, third and fourth qualities, each being kept separate in the subsequent stages of processing.

While I was in Nyasaland experiments were being carried out in neighbouring estate factories to improve the withering and rolling stages of tea production. The aim was, and still is, a continuous flow process which can embrace all the stages of manufacture and many improvements are constantly being achieved. African tea plantations, particularly the new ones, have the most advanced tea-processing methods in the world. Probably the biggest innovation in recent years has been the use of the Rotorvane, which has largely replaced the batch-process tea-roller as a continuous processing machine in its own right. The Rotorvane distorts the leaf and bursts the cells without loss of juice or rise in temperature, giving a more complete oxidization.

The next stage, oxidization, usually referred to as fermentation, starts as the leaf is broken up in the rollers and may take from twenty minutes to three hours. In the fermenting room the different qualities are thinly spread on trays stacked on racks so that the oxidization of polyphenols and formation of oils, which give the tea its flavour and aroma, may continue. When some way is found of improving on the batch system of fermentation it may at last be possible for tea to be processed from beginning to end completely automatically, with conveyor belts linking the various stages of manufacture.

Drying, also known as firing, follows. The moist tea is fed on to trays slowly travelling from top to bottom in a large drying chamber, through which hot air is forced by a fan in a continuous flow from a furnace. This takes about thirty minutes, according to the moisture content; the tea then comes out of the drier and could be used to drink. But before becoming the finished article each quality of leaf, originally separated in the green-leaf sifting stage, is now sorted into different sizes known as leaf grades, broken grades, fannings and dust. These categories are then meticulously sorted to give grade sizes referred to by abbreviated terms:

Qualities	Leaf	Brokens	Fannings	Dust
1st	F.O.P.	F.B.O.P.	F.B.O.P.F.	
2nd	O.P.	B.O.P.	B.O.P.F.	No. 1
3rd	P.	B.P.	P.F.	
4th	P.S.	B.P.S.	F.	No. 2

The meanings of the leaf grade abbreviations are F for Flowery, O for Orange, P for Pekoe and S for Souchong, and these terms originated from names used by the Chinese for their own grades, some being direct translations and others corruptions. The Chinese term *Pei Hao* means 'white down' and is the name given to the delicate flavour of tea made from young leaf buds covered with whitish down, but Pekoe, the English corruption of this term, does not, on the London market today, necessarily refer to the downy growth of the leaf buds, but generally indicates a bold leaf size. Flowery is a translation of the Chinese words *Tsai Haui*, and again dates from the days when green tea scented with flowers was still extensively drunk in England, though today, with teas from India, Ceylon and Africa, the word 'orange' is an indication of quality and has no connection with flavouring whatever. Souchong is a corruption of the Chinese words *Hsiao Chung*, meaning 'small sort', but today it has come to mean a well-rolled leaf, rarely used in proprietary blends.

Through the years the larger leaf grades have lost their popularity in England in favour of the broken and fannings grades which are quicker infusing and give a strong brew with thickness of body and good colour. They are also more suitable for packing in the proprietary brand packets and, as in most factories in Nyasaland, these were the main grades manufactured on Thornwood.

The letter B stands for broken and explains exactly what has been done to the leaf grade. The fannings are smaller than the brokens and F denotes that they have been sieved from, or fanned out, as often used to be the case, from the broken grades. Dust, sifted from both the brokens and fannings, is the smallest grade produced, and is useful as strong, quick-infusing tea. It is always popular with caterers, and has now established itself as the natural grade, with small fannings, for putting into tea bags. In spite of its unattractive name, dust, particularly that which comes from the first two leaves and bud, i.e. first-quality tea, is often very good tea indeed.

It should be explained that in the tea trade of Western Europe 'tea' always implies black tea. Green tea, which was the first tea to arrive there from China 300 years ago, is now virtually unknown outside oriental restaurants, although it is still grown by the Chinese and Japanese for their own consumption. Some is exported to North Africa, where it is still drunk quite extensively.

Green tea is unfermented tea. The Chinese used to steam the tea during the withering stage and then roll and fire it three times, by which time the leaves were a bluish green instead of dark brown or black. Green teas were much prized, and some of them, not necessarily the best, had jasmine, gardenia, orange blossom and magnolia added to them for scent. The teas were put into chests, hot from the final firing, and freshly plucked flowers were strewn over every two-inch layer. The next day the mixture was poured on to trays and toasted for an hour or two and then re-packed into chests, with or without the flowers sifted out.

Oolong, or semi-fermented tea, was a speciality of Formosa and had some of the characteristics of both black and green tea. Green, black and oolong were the three categories of tea many years ago, but nowadays all the most important trade is in black tea.

As the quality of the different grades varies from day to day in manufacture, individual grades are bulked prior to despatch to ensure evenness of quality, after which they are packed in 60 lb. or 110 lb. chests and a consignment is made up usually comprising 100 to 200 chests. Consignments are despatched regularly throughout the season, and on arrival in London, tea is sold under a mark, usually of the plantation on which it was grown.

Like Ceylon, Nyasaland was originally a coffee-producing country, and indeed so bright was its future that a coffee bush in full bearing was the coat of arms of the Protectorate, as it was then. However, it was evident by 1902 that, because of blight, coffee was not going to live up to its promise, and attention was turned to tea, which was successfully introduced in 1886 and 1888 when tea from Kew and the Royal Botanical Gardens, Edinburgh, was taken to the Blantyre Mission of the Church of Scotland.

In 1891 Henry Brown, an ex-Ceylon planter, sowed tea seeds in Mlanje on the coffee gardens at Lauderdale and Thornwood. Little attention was given to the plants for some years, but as the coffee began to fail, care was taken to gather every tea seed and these were planted in nurseries. The seedlings were duly set out and from these developed the commercial growing of tea in Mlanje. Henry Brown died in 1920 and his Thornwood garden continued to be managed by his wife and daughter up to 1945, when both died within a short time, and Thornwood, known as Brown's Old Estate, was bought by the Rosehaugh group of companies.

For the first few weeks I was put up by another young assistant who lived in what had formerly been the Browns' old guest house, but at last a new bungalow was built for me in a magnificent position on top of a hill with views of Mlanje Mountain. A patch of tea bushes had to be pulled up to make room for it, and I uprooted a few more to make the garden bigger. I took cuttings of the many English and local plants in the Browns' old garden and before the end of the first year my own garden was making a fine show. The bungalow was about the size of a suburban bungalow in England and was furnished with necessary basic furniture, most of which had been put together by the estate carpenter. I bought china and provisions from the store ten miles down the road, and my curtains were made up from material chosen from the Indian duka. My new home was a bit bare, but very clean and undoubtedly a palace compared with what young planters might have expected in previous generations. It was usually free from lizards, snakes and other tropical creatures which frequently got into the older buildings, though I used many tins of fly spray to keep away mosquitoes.

Plantation bungalows in Africa did not have the exotic touches of their older counterparts in India and Ceylon where there was a rich local culture to colour their Victorian opulence, but I had a cook, a houseboy and a gardener, which made life very comfortable.

After Christmas the manager went on leave and I settled down to my work in the factory, arriving there at 5.30 a.m. to call over the labour and allocate their various tasks. It often happened that the leaf gathered the previous day would be sufficiently withered before I left the factory for breakfast at eight o'clock to start the rolling process of manufacture. I would return to the factory, and until noon the later stages, such as green-leaf sorting, fermenting and firing, would have begun. About noon, as I went for lunch, the early-morning pluckings of green leaf would begin to arrive at the factory and labour would be made available, under a capitoe, to spread the leaf on the racks for withering. I usually slept until 2 p.m. before going back to the factory, when work would begin on washing down the rollers and fermenting tables.

The most wonderful time of the day was undoubtedly sundown, particularly during the rainy season between October and April, when from my bungalow I could look over the colourful garden and lawn towards Mlanje and my favourite view, the Ruo Waterfall.

As grading and sifting went on continuously for twenty-four hours a day, I would visit the factory after dinner and again during the night to see that everything was in order. Walking through the tea bushes on pitch-black nights could be an eerie experience, but on other nights the whole of Mlanje would be illuminated by lightning, and this, with the sound of crashing thunder, scared me more than once. The mountain was notorious for its own particular form of bad weather called a 'chiperone'. This was a mixture of cold mist and drenching rain which could descend without warning on unsuspecting travellers and maroon them for days. Anyone caught in a chiperone on the mountain had the choice of trying to get below it, with the risk of falling into gorges thousands of feet deep, or staying put and dying of exposure. Chiperones usually lasted for five days and the Africans were as scared of them as they were of the leopards which roamed over the mountain. The only people who lived for any length of time on the mountain were the forestry officers whose job was to look after the great forests of Mlanje cedars. These were not really cedars at all, but a unique and incredibly ancient sort of conifer which provide the only ant-resistant wood in Africa. They are full of a thick, yellow resin which preserves them and give out a wonderful smell which pervades the whole mountain. Because there is a constant danger to them from fire, they are under the protection of the Colonial Forestry Service.

Tea planters work very long hours during the season, and the non-manufacturing periods are spent overhauling the machinery. They are also great innovators and competition between the estates to improve their manufacturing methods is very keen. But, even so, like all Europeans in tropical agriculture, they find time for recreation at their clubs. I first visited the Mlanje Club with George one evening during my first week on the estate. It was near to the Boma by that part of the mountain which rises steeply from the road, and following George in through the side door into the small, narrow bar, the scene which greeted me was unlike anything I had ever seen before.

Sitting on high stools along the counter, in an atmosphere heavy with tobacco smoke, was a group of the most sun-tanned white men I had ever met. Two lights shone down from rather dilapidated painted lanterns, and behind the counter, wearing a white kanzu, was a particularly black-skinned African. The only form of amusement was conversation, and as they talked the planters drank, smoked and munched peanuts, carefully separating them from the sausage flies which circled the lanterns and then fell, roasted and half-dead, into the bowls. To an avid reader of Somerset Maugham and John Buchan the club was a disappointment. On the five-mile drive back George told me that during the plucking and heavy manufacturing period it was usual to go to the club once a week, but during the dry season, when less tea was made, the club came into its own for tennis, cricket and golf, and was the centre for the social functions of the district. Since I left Mlanje a new club has been built which is much more splendid and bears no resemblance to the one that I knew.

Before the manager went away I had my first experience of tea-tasting, as the usual practice was to taste the individual grades of tea from each consignment for leaf and liquor before it was despatched. Samples were also kept back from consignments sent to London to compare with reports sent out by the company's brokers in London. I was so enthusiastic about tasting that I got the houseboy at my bungalow to brew endless pots of tea for me, which I tasted sitting on the kondi. I was able to discern between thickness and thinness of body in the various grades, and pick out teas having poor taste due to faulty manufacture, but I was no expert.

After the manager returned from his leave it was arranged that I should also work in the gardens. I learnt that most tea bushes are grown from seeds, rather like nutmegs in appearance, taken from seed bearers. These are cultivated solely for that purpose, being left unpruned and allowed to reach their full height of about thirty to forty feet. These seeds are sown in carefully prepared nursery beds and tended until they are strong enough for transplanting. From these beds the young plants are removed to their permanent

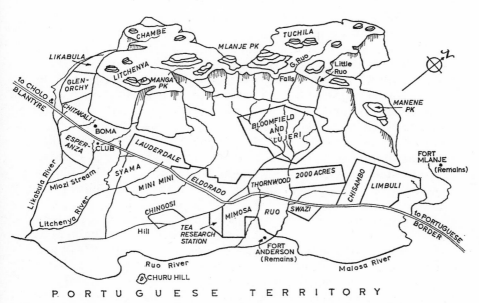

The tea estates on Mount Mlanje (from a sketch by the author).

position in the gardens where they are planted two or three feet
apart in rows, several thousand to the acre. New plants are also
raised from cuttings. These are invariably identical with the parent
plant, and they avoid some of the problems of variation from type
which arise as a result of hybridization, but the nurseries of seedlings
are necessary so that the best plants can be selected to improve the
strain.

Depending upon whether the bush is grown at a low altitude in
hot, moist conditions or on the high mountain slopes to produce a
better quality, tea takes between two and a half and five years to
become fully productive and mature. The life of a tea bush is about
fifty years. It is pruned once every two to four years, again according
to altitude, in order to keep its size down to about three feet and
create a flat top to the bush, known as a table, to make plucking
easier.

The pluckers move round the garden from section to section, and
the leaf plucked from each is sent to the factory daily. By the time
all sections have been completed, the first bushes plucked have had
time to grow a new flush, and the plucking round starts again. In
the past, bushes used to be planted in rows down the hillsides, but
because much top soil was lost in this way they are now planted in
contours, and elaborate drainage systems are prepared on new
clearings before the tea is planted to prevent soil erosion.

Not having given much attention before to what went on outside
the factory, I was quite surprised at the different types of work that
had to be done in the garden. Besides pruning, bushes are manured
and sprayed with insecticide and the weeds cleared away from
around them. They have to be watched carefully for signs of ill-
health, such as blister blight or one of the root diseases which are a
very serious matter. In an area where tea is intensively cultivated
an infection can quickly spread from one plantation to the next.
The labour is split into gangs for carrying out the various tasks, like
tending to nurseries, clearing forests for new planting sites, splitting
logs for factory fuel, sawing timber and making bricks. Others
maintain estate roads and bridges, while carpenters, builders and
mechanics work at various tasks throughout the estate.

It was customary in most of the producing companies for assistants to spend three periods of three to four years on the various
gardens belonging to the company so that they would get field and
factory experience. They were then ready to become assistant
managers and ultimately managers. After many years a manager
might return to the United Kingdom to become a director of the
company, or, if not choosing to return, could become a visiting

agent for an overseas agency house, representing estate owners in the producing country where an intimate knowledge of local estates is valuable.

While I was still on the bottom rung of this ladder in the autumn of 1952, producers were having difficulty selling their teas above the cost of production, which was around 3s. (15p) per pound. The sudden demand which was expected to follow de-rationing in Great Britain had not materialised and as the crop from North India, the largest supplier of teas to the United Kingdom, became available for sale on the London auctions, the average price for these teas fell from 3s. 8d. (18p) towards the end of 1951 to 3s. (15p) in the early months of 1952, bringing about slump selling conditions affecting other producing countries.

Although this was known on the estates, it was brought home to me in reality one morning when, returning to the bungalow on my motor-bike for breakfast, I was sent for by the manager, who had received a cable from home saying that the company had to retrench generally. The labour force was to be reduced, and work on the new clearings and buildings was to be suspended. I went to see Mr. Bishop after breakfast and he told me with regret that the company were giving me three months' notice, for, as the most junior and most recent member of the staff to join the estate, my salary was one of the expenses to be saved. I made arrangements to leave for England by sea from Beira on the Mozambique coast.

The low price of tea and world over-production is a continuing problem for areas producing medium-quality tea, and is still not solved at the beginning of the 1970's. However, I was glad to see recently from a directory of tea estates in Africa that many of the people I met in Nyasaland are still there, and George Forrest is now manager of the Kasembereka Estate in the Cholo district not far from Mlanje.

C

2

Tasting Tea in London

Leaving Nyasaland seemed a setback at the time, but I realized that this move could give me the opportunity of working in another section of the tea trade. After I had time to consider my future I thought I would try to get some training as a tea taster in London where I could learn about teas from every part of the world.

Most of the tea which comes into the London auctions is bought by the big national blending and packing companies, who sell it under proprietary brands in retail quarter-pound packets. I decided I would be wise to try to get my initial training as a taster with one of these companies rather than with an estate producing company, agency house or tea broker. After all, it is the blenders who have to have a really comprehensive knowledge of the world's tea, and I wanted to learn how they tasted and selected them.

In reply to my letters, Brooke Bond asked me to complete an application form, but Lyons gave me an appointment straight away, and I went to be interviewed by one of the directors at their blending and packing factory in Greenford, Middlesex. The most important part of Lyons Tea Department is a room thirty yards long with a white-tiled floor, a glass roof and parallel counters running from end to end on which were hundreds of pots and bowls with lids, and sample tins of tea for tasting. Women were hustling around the room arranging and weighing and wheeling spittoons away for emptying. At counters in different parts of the room were groups of buyers and blenders with their assistants, tasting the teas.

Seeking out the most senior man in the Tea and Coffee Department, I explained why I was there and answered all the usual questions about my past and hobbies. Then I was handed over to an assistant buyer who showed me round the tasting room and explained briefly the procedure for tasting tea. Back in the office I was asked what I thought of the tasting room and replied that it had impressed me very much, whereupon I was told the directors would be writing to let me know whether they had an opening for me.

A few days later I received a letter accepting me as a pupil taster on twelve months' probation, and within two weeks I was at work. On the first day I was introduced to the buyers, blenders and junior assistants, and told to do nothing much but walk round the tasting room to absorb the atmosphere and see what goes on in the tasting room of a tea-buying and -blending department and to learn as much as possible without getting in anyone's way.

I recall one of the blenders selecting two bowls of tea from the number of proprietary blends he was tasting, and telling me that one was a quality packet and the other an inferior blend. He asked me to taste the two teas to find out whether I could tell the difference. I picked up a spoon and self-consciously sipped from each bowl. It seemed to me that one, if I could have had some sugar in it, would have been a delightfully thick and strong cup of tea, while the other tasted weak, so I chose the first as the good tea. Like most people after years of rationing, I thought that a good tea was one which produced the strongest brew from the fewest spoonfuls. The blender told me I was wrong, saying that it would take me many months before I began to appreciate a blend made from quality rather than plain teas.

I noticed that to establish the value of tea, not only was the liquor tasted, but the dry leaf and infused leaf were examined by sight, touch and by smell. Tasting is largely a matter of comparison, and it is essential when tasting a number of teas together, known as a batch, for each one to be brewed in exactly the same way: an equal weight of tea; an equal quantity of freshly boiled water; equal time for brewing; equal size and style of pot and bowl (the pot being the equivalent of a household teapot, the bowl being the teacup).

The amount of tea measured and weighed out is governed by the size of the pot; for small sizes the equivalent weight of a farthing is usual, and for larger pots half an old pennyweight. Brooke Bond traditionally use an old shilling or 5·65 grams. In India the coin used to be a silver four-anna piece. The correct amount of tea having been weighed into each pot, freshly drawn water is brought to the boil and added as quickly as possible, filling each pot, which is then covered with the lid. The tea is allowed to brew for either five or six minutes and after the infusion is completed, the pots, with the lids still in place, are tipped so that the liquid drains off between the pot and lid into the bowl. The infused leaf is tipped on to the reverse side of the lids and placed on top of the pots. This means that the bowls are now full of tea and the infused and dry leaf are ready for examination. The taster proceeds to taste the liquid and smell the infusion, noting the colour of both and comparing them with that of the dry leaf. He takes a spoonful from the bowl which he is tasting, quickly sucks the tea on to the taste buds at the back of his tongue, and after a second or two, in which time his palate has completely registered the tea, he spits it out into a big spittoon on wheels.

Buyers rarely taste on their own, they usually have an assistant with whom they check the characteristics of each tea and estimates of its value. The taste of a tea cannot be photographed or tape-recorded, but a taster will remember it for years with complete accuracy. Having a second trained palate to record it is the only way of making a 'carbon copy'.

A batch of teas for tasting will consist of those teas with a known or pre-assessed value called 'standards', against which the teas to be valued are compared. The taster, in valuing the tea, will first taste a standard, having a spoonful of tea to be valued immediately ready for taking into his mouth after he has spat the mouthful of standard into the spittoon. This ensures that he compares the two teas in the shortest possible time, and is in fact the only way of making an accurate judgment of a tea, although an experienced trained taster, with one tasting alone of an unvalued tea, can often assess its merits and value it to the nearest penny on the ruling rate of the market.

It was explained to me that teas were tasted with milk because some have a better colour than others when milk has been added, and as most of the general public drink their tea with milk this is a most important factor in determining a tea's value. The milk is put in the tasting bowls before the tea is added, rather than after-wards. By doing it this way there is less chance of the milk being scalded because at the initial moment of contact there is more milk than tea, and it mixes more easily with the tea as it is added. Also it is easier to judge how much milk is being put in. So if I am pressed to take sides in the eternal dispute as to whether the milk or the tea goes in first, I am with the 'milk first' supporters.

The system for training tasters at Lyons was, and no doubt still is, to taste several times a day, every day of the working year, small batches of about twelve teas chosen to include three growths with prominent flavours, such as Assam from north-east India, Darjeeling from the foothills of the Himalayas and the high-grown teas from Ceylon. I was soon able to distinguish between Assam teas with their thick type of body, and strong, malty taste, the fine quality of Darjeelings with their distinctive blackcurrant and muscatel flavour, and the aromatic flavours of the high-grown Nuwara Eliya, Dimbula and Uva teas from Ceylon.

Apart from this, I learnt in time that these teas have a different style and colour of dry leaf, which shows up also in the infusions. The Assam teas, produced early in the season, have a fine golden-tippy appearance, and later in the season, when there is less tip available, they take on a grey, rather than black, appearance. Ceylon leaf, by contrast, frequently has an attractive black colouring, often with a bluish tinge. The manner in which the teas react to

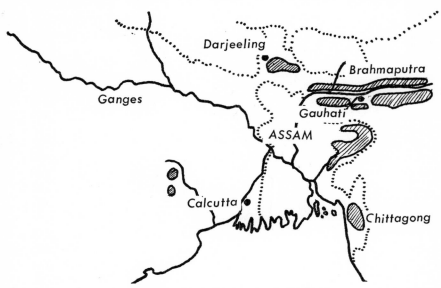

The tea-growing areas of north-east India.

milk also gives a clue as to their origins. The liquor of the Darjeeling teas has a greyish appearance, Assams a bright red-brown colour and the Ceylons are bright golden.

After a few months I was expected to be able to tell, by tasting, the area from which each tea in the batch had come, without knowing which teas had been brewed and without seeing the dry leaf. If the teas were of really fine quality it was possible to identify every one of a 'blind' batch of twelve teas correctly, but later, when less expensive teas were used, and even with greater experience, the task became more difficult as the individual flavour and colour of the liquors with milk became less prominent. Even so, a taster with long experience would have no difficulty at all in telling the growth even of the very lowest quality. Occasionally tasters of many years' experience would prepare batches for me, and in their efforts to confuse me would select certain well-known gardens which, although of one growth, had tasting characteristics of another. Such teas are rare, but if included in a batch could make correct individual identification very difficult.

It is almost impossible for members of the general public to understand the remarkable sensitivity of a trained palate. Someone given two very similar teas to taste at home will probably say first that he cannot detect any difference. He will taste them again and

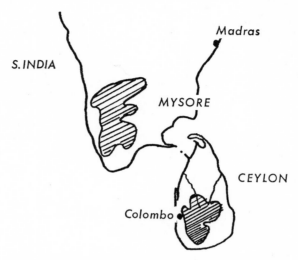

The tea-growing areas of South India and Ceylon.

say perhaps one is a bit stronger than the other. The third time he will decide perhaps they do taste the same after all. But to a trained taster the two teas will each have an identity which could not be confused with any other tea. There was always room for discussion on the valuation or usefulness of a tea, but its description or even the degree of variation in the quality of two shipments of the same tea was always accepted as undisputed fact in the same way that a musician identifies the pitch of a note beyond question. Years later when I worked with trained tasters from China I found they judged teas by exactly the same methods, and although their ideas of quality for the British market were different, there was never any disagreement over the tasting characteristics of a tea.

Having had practical experience of the grades made by one African factory, I was particularly intrigued at now being able to see grades made by factories in a variety of producing countries, and was surprised to find how easily buyers could distinguish between similar teas within the leaf, broken and fannings grades, even recognising teas from certain gardens on their appearance. I realized that a 'tea maker' on one garden, while knowing the quality of his own teas, often had no means of knowing how his teas compared with other gardens either from the same or other tea-growing areas.

The lids of sampling tins were always replaced immediately after use, so as to preserve the tea's quality. It is for this reason that tea, after manufacture, is stored and packed in containers which, although not completely air-tight, prevent the flavour of the tea escaping, and protect it from dampness and contamination from other odours which would spoil it.

A simple test to illustrate how tea depreciates in quality if left uncovered is to take two samples of the same tea, place each in separate tins, leave the lid off one overnight and the next morning brew the two teas separately. The tea which was exposed to the air will have lost much of its strength, body and flavour. Tea which is properly protected will keep quite successfully for many months and its keeping merits are of considerable importance to the blenders.

As I became more confident in dealing with test batches, I was keen to find out what was going on around me. The tasting department was divided into two buying sections, one for North Indian, Pakistan and African teas, the other for Ceylon, South Indian and Indonesian. There was also, of course, the blending section. Both the buying sections bought teas from the auctions held in London each week; the Ceylon and South Indian teas were sold on Tuesdays, and North Indian, African, Indonesian and other parts of the world on Mondays and Wednesdays, totalling altogether between 60,000 and 80,000 chests per week.

Teas for sale in London are being landed from many countries all the time in consignments from the individual factories, and from North India alone come several hundred gardens bearing estate names, in the same way that Thornwood was one of many in Nyasaland. Each consignment from a factory may be made up of just one brokens and one fannings grade, or it may consist of more than one quality of each type.

The tea-producing companies bringing their teas to London for selling in the auctions arrange for them to be handled by selling brokers who act as auctioneers. There are several firms of selling brokers who sell the teas, either by auction or privately, and when the teas are landed each broker arranges to have the teas he is handling checked for uniformity of quality. The drawing of samples accounts for the small circle of metal or 'bung' to be seen in the sides of tea chests.

The brokers then arrange to have one chest of each grade from one garden invoice opened and placed in a room in the warehouse where the teas are put on show, allowing samples of all offerings for sale in any one week to be drawn by any company interested in the tea. For this they use the Tea Clearing House, opened in 1952 with offices and a warehouse in London, where all buyers and brokers submit the numbers of each tea they require. The Tea Clearing House, having all the applications, distributes them to each wharf where the teas are lying, enabling the wharves to draw all samples at one time and pass them to the Tea Clearing House to await collection by the applicants at their convenience. This procedure does away with the necessity for any company wanting samples having to send their messengers to each of the wharves, which are spread over a large area on either side of the Thames.

Each selling broker makes up catalogues for the teas he is selling and all the catalogues for the week's sales printed by the Tea Brokers' Association are distributed to the buyers and brokers. Each selling broker, having valued the teas in his catalogue, will pass his price ideas for each tea to prospective buyers before the auctions, though naturally the buyers are not over-influenced by the selling broker's indications and rely on their own judgment in assessing the teas' value. The senior buyers and blenders of the big tea companies are very highly paid men, but by shrewd buying and anticipation of market movement they can save many times their year's salary for their company. Indeed, it was often said that the profits of the blending firms are obtained more on the ability to buy than the ability to sell the tea.

Samples received by the blenders of teas being offered in the auctions are sorted into origin, grade and sometimes valuation order. The individual grades of each mark are tasted against the same grades of the same mark from the preceding invoice, offered in the previous week's auctions, thereby allowing any change in quality to be more easily observed. For example, if a Thornwood B.O.P. sold at 4s. (20p) one week and the market remained steady, this same grade of tea, with a slight improvement in quality, might realise a slightly higher price by a penny or so in the following week's sale, depending upon the extent of the competition among buyers for the improved quality.

At Lyons, all offerings are first tasted by the assistant buyers, who make as accurate a price assessment as possible of the value of the teas likely to be suitable for the company's requirements. These are called 'plums', while the unsuitable teas are known as the 'pups'. Having been valued, the teas are tasted again, this time by the senior buyers, who confirm or alter, if necessary, the valuation given by the juniors and perhaps reject further teas. This procedure provides an excellent training for assistant buyers without their having too soon to accept the responsibility of actually buying the teas in the auctions.

Within the year I was put in the Indian buying section, adding considerably to the interest of my work, as I could taste and study in detail teas from North India, which provides the largest range available from one area, having within it the main producing districts of Assam, Darjeeling, Dooars and Terai, each with hundreds of different gardens. Joining the buying section also gave me a chance of seeing the other African teas from Uganda, Kenya, Tanganyika, Portuguese East Africa and the Belgian Congo.

Although the ultimate value of a tea is determined by tasting, it certainly appeared that half the evidence for valuing the teas is in what can be learned from their appearance. I saw that the tasters would examine the dry leaf to see whether it was hard and well rolled, indicating a well-made tea with good keeping qualities, as against a spongy or flaky tea of poorer quality, and that red fibre in the leaf does not necessarily mean that the tea is of poor quality. The infused leaf is also significant. A bright coppery colour denotes quality, a dark or dull one is inferior and a very black infused leaf usually indicates that the tea is sour or out of condition. There is a similarity between the colour of the infused leaf and the colour of the liquor with milk. A dull type of infusion gives a dull liquor, a brighter infusion gives a brighter liquor, while a greenish infusion, rather than the desired coppery colour, produces a greenish liquor with a harsh taste.

Terms such as 'harsh', 'greenish' and 'flavour' meant little to me at first in the sense that they applied to tea, but I learnt that they were often accounted for by seasonal variations in the producing countries. Teas produced in North India at the beginning of the season are known as 'new season's' teas and frequently have a rubbery or raw taste. The first or second flush teas of good, bright colour give flavour, aroma, and are brisk, described by tasters as having 'point', while rich, ripe, round or smooth teas are all termed 'full'. Certain second-flush Assam teas are known as 'greenfly', for at this time of the year, as the name implies, the bushes are attacked by greenfly. But, surprisingly enough, these insects give the tea an unusual but attractive flavour!

Teas manufactured in the heavy rains are often known as 'weathery', describing an unpleasant taste brought about by the humidity which is not conducive to good manufacture, as the teas tend to absorb excess moisture. After the 'rains' teas, when humidity gives way to better manufacturing conditions, come the distinctive quality and flavoury autumnal teas. After this the teas tend to lose their quality due to insufficient sun and rain and are known as 'end-of-season make'.

Quality variations take place in all tea-producing countries due to seasonal weather changes, but the manner in which the tea is manufactured also has a decided influence on quality. Over-withering, over-oxidization or incorrect firing sometimes give dull brownish liquors which are not clear or bright, or flat or soft liquors, lacking in briskness and pungency; fruity-tasting teas suggest a taint due to over-oxidization or perhaps a bacterially infected floor, while harsh liquors which are bitter suggest under-withering, under-oxidization, but more generally under-rolling, and bakey, burnt, high-fired or stewed teas are all caused by inappropriate firing.

Teas, being very hydroscopic, are also susceptible to contamination by such things as oil, soap, fruit and even on occasions the wooden chests in which they are packed, so giving taints to the liquors which are detrimental to the flavour of the tea. We often had orange tea, and one day we even found a banana tea!

Buyers place their bids through buying brokers. These brokers tasted and valued all the teas selling in the auctions for any one week, and, irrespective of the price indication given by the selling broker, passed on their own judgment as to the teas' value to their clients. The buyers, after considering the selling brokers' and buying brokers' ideas of the likely price and comparing them with their own valuation based on tasting, would decide they wanted certain teas and either telephone the bids through to their buying broker before the sale, and then attend the auctions themselves to adjust those bids in the case of a fluctuating market, or, alternatively, they would submit their bids to the buying broker in the auction room as and when the teas came up for sale.

A buyer wishing to buy as much as 5,000 chests of certain qualities makes sure he has bids on suitable teas in excess of this quantity, as there are bound to be other buyers interested in some of the same teas who might well be prepared to make higher bids than himself. Further, if other blenders found that one buyer was particularly anxious to get a certain tea and seemingly had no limit, there is the chance they would intentionally bid against him.

In a large blending company a buyer is able to taste on a Friday, in readiness for Monday's auctions, as many as 800 teas, representing about 40,000 chests, each usually sipped twice. Strangely enough, after tasting so many teas, one's palate does not become dull, but, if anything, more acute, although one does become physically

tired due to standing for hours, and mentally tired by the concentration needed to give adequate attention to each tea.

My opportunity to visit the auctions soon came, and I was told
to be at the buying broker's office in Mincing Lane to await the
arrival of our buyer in time for the auctions at 10.30 a.m. The tea
auctions were at that time held in Plantation House, which was
built between 1935 and 1938 to provide a centre for produce dealing
in the City, and the Tea Auditorium was on the seventh and eighth
floors. It was opened in 1937, just a hundred years after the first
tea from India was auctioned, and had an impressive mansard-type
roof twenty-one feet high designed to give room for raised seating for
250 people. Special attention had been given to the acoustics, the
walls were made of acoustic slabs and the auctioneer's rostrum had
been moved more than once to find the best position. It was covered
by a canopy like a church-pulpit sounding board. Around the room
were shields bearing the brightly coloured coats of arms of the various
producing countries, and the ceiling was glass-panelled, suggesting
that the room was open to the sky.

The room gradually filled with buyers, including those of the
other big blending companies, and buying brokers who sat each at
his accustomed place.

At exactly half past ten the auctioneer, a senior member of the
firm of selling brokers making the first offerings, took his place on
the rostrum and teas were sold before I was aware the auction had
begun. It was incredible. The bids came in so fast that it was some
time before I was able to pick out the prices at which the auctioneer
started the bidding for each tea as it was offered, and the advanced
bids made by the buying brokers in farthings, halfpennies or pennies.

Bids from the buying brokers to the auctioneer came very quickly
and ceased abruptly, and, with a small tap of the gavel, bidding for
the next lot started immediately. On occasions there may appear
to be little bidding; but this does not mean there is no competition,
for each buying broker might have several bids in his catalogues for
the same teas, some of them being too low to be submitted. By
watching carefully, I was able to notice buyers giving bids to their
buying brokers, the communication perhaps being a nod, a slight
lift of the pen or a nudge.

A 'lot' of tea usually comprises anything between eighteen to
forty-eight chests, and as it is common practice to divide lots between
two or more buyers, one buying broker may often be heard calling
to another who has the bidding, 'I want some', meaning that he is
prepared to negotiate a split. As soon as a buying broker has outbid
his competitors and agreement has been reached as to the manner

in which the lot shall be split, the selling broker declares the tea sold. The division of lots in this way is not a device to enable buyers to keep down the price, but rather to allow buyers needing only small quantities to get a share of any tea in the sale. The length of time taken to complete an auction is governed not only by the quantity of tea available for sale but also the state of the market. If the demand is good, sales are made more easily and speedily, but if poor, the auctioneer tries to encourage sales and naturally this takes longer. Sometimes during the winter months, when there are large offerings of tea from North India, the auctions may go on until late in the evenings.

During the sale, buyers keep a running total of purchases made and at the end of the day I was astounded to discover that my company had bought over 5,000 chests, worth £100,000. A day or so after the auctions the buying brokers send a one-pound sample of each tea bought to the buyers, so that they can taste them and record their liquor quality before entering the tea into stock to await use in the blends as and when they are needed. The selling brokers earn 1% commission on all teas which pass through their hands and the buying brokers ½%. To fulfil their blending requirements, many packing companies buy not only in London but also in the auctions in Calcutta, Colombo, Cochin and Nairobi.

At first it might appear that blending is unnecessary, and that it would be less costly if the public were able to receive their teas direct from the individual gardens. In fact, some teas are sold in this way, but the disadvantage of doing so is that it is impossible to procure a constant quality throughout the year. Teas from individual gardens vary not only throughout the season but also from one season to the next, due to local climatic conditions, and in some areas the manufacturing season is short. But by buying adequate quantities from different growths and gardens and blending them together, the tea companies can create blends which maintain a constant quality and price from one month to the next so far as market prices allow.

The varied leaf and liquoring characteristics of the individual growths, district and marks are all used in such proportions as to get the maximum benefit from each. Assam teas of orthodox manufacture are extremely useful for all blending purposes, as they have the virtues of good appearance, a strong, malty flavour and they make an ideal base for a blend. The term 'orthodox Assam' is used to mean teas made by the same method of processing as that described in the previous chapter, and to distinguish them from those now made in Assam by what is known as the C.T.C. process. This is an abbreviation meaning crushing, tearing and curling the leaf by passing it, after withering and possibly a short, orthodox roll, through a C.T.C. machine which has two horizontal four-foot rollers with stainless-steel cutting segments working on the principle of a mangle, one revolving at one-tenth the speed of the other. This process produces teas with a strong, coloury liquor which are the basis of the quick-brew blends introduced in the early 1950's.

The Dooars district produces teas having smooth, mellow, full-bodied liquors of good colour, and they help to bind together all the teas used in a blend, though some of these teas are made by a process which differs from the orthodox method and are known as Legg-cut teas. In this process, leaf which has received insufficient wither is compressed and cut into strips, after which it is rolled. The autumnal teas from this district have a distinctive flavour and strength unique in character.

Darjeelings are renowned for their muscatel flavour and aroma; the high-grown Ceylons, from districts where the leaf grows slowly, have an incomparable fragrance, fine flavour and rich golden colour; and there is always a good demand for mid-country Ceylons with their full, rich, flavoury liquors.

South Indian tea, especially when grown in the higher districts of Tranvancore and Nilgiri, have an aromatic quality much sought after in certain markets. Other districts provide useful, bright-liquoring medium teas, but without the fullness of North Indian varieties, and are sometimes used in blends in place of similar-tasting Ceylons.

Indonesian teas from Java and Sumatra are consistent in quality and appearance throughout the year, and the high-grown teas from these growths have a flavour somewhat similar to those from corresponding elevations in South India and Ceylon. African teas are being used in blends in greater quantities as their quality improves year by year.

After the basic requirements of body, flavour, pungency and colour have been met, it may be found that the blend is averaging out at too high a price, and to counteract this, quantities of neutral, sound-quality teas are added, known as fillers, which will not damage the character and flavour of the blend. These are available from most growths, particularly the marginal districts of North India and Africa, the low-grown teas from Ceylon, and teas from Indonesia and the Argentine. They usually have a good black leaf and coloury liquors, but without any distinctive flavour. Although fillers are regular components and necessary to blends, they must be used with discretion. An excessive proportion would detract from the strength, body and flavour, thereby wasting the qualities of the expensive teas.

As there is a variation in tea from different growths and gardens, so water varies in different parts of the country and teas react differently to them. Packers take this into account when blending, and draw samples of water for test purposes from the areas in which their blends will be sold, to make sure that the most appropriate teas are blended for each district.

Soft water, usually of moorland or surface origin, is found in Lancashire, Yorkshire, Wales, Scotland and some parts of south-west England, while water containing varying proportions of temporary and permanent hardness from underground supplies, known as alkaline and non-alkaline types, is generally found in the south. In the London area, for example, the water is approximately four-fifths temporary and one-fifth permanent.

In soft-water areas it is usual to use heavy, thick liquoring teas, such as orthodox-manufactured malty Assam and Java teas; soft water brings out the best in them; indeed, even poorer-quality teas from the same growths would benefit. There are, however, certain teas which are unsuitable in these areas for a variety of reasons. China Keemun, Darjeeling, high-grown Ceylon and South Indian teas have a tendency to lose their bouquet; C.T.C. and Legg-cut become brassy; Japanese and China green teas react unfavourably; and thin liquoring teas are wasted. It follows, therefore, that the latter teas derive the utmost benefit from hard water, while on the thick liquoring teas hard water has the reverse effect of not bringing out their strength.

Small packers blending for specific districts take into account the nature of the water and blend accordingly, but a good blender should be able to produce a good all-round blend to a specific price which will brew well in any water.

The public takes for granted the fact that it can buy packets of tea at the same price week after week, and even year after year, without appreciating how much work this entails. For apart from the variations in quality, blenders must also take into account fluctuations in availability and rises and falls in prices. Then it is vital to know which teas to blend together. Particular care has to be taken with teas of fine quality, as it would be a waste to blend two very stringent teas together. For example, a very fine Assam with a very fine Ceylon would mean only that one would detract from the other, so it follows that the better-quality blends have a pronounced flavour of one of the main growths only and many of the packers accordingly label their blends Indian, Ceylon or Darjeeling.

The same principle of good basic blending applies equally to the less expensive, medium- and low-quality packets, for although in these schedules the high-priced flavoury teas are not added, these blends still have the attributes of body, strength, flavour and colour which result from good all-round blending. Preference for one company's tea rather than another's is purely a matter of personal taste. Blenders make every effort to maintain a constant standard, and ensure that the public is given teas which are comparable to those of their competitors by tasting each other's blends all the time.

All the experience and knowledge of the world's tea supplies, buying and blending, go for nothing unless tea is correctly prepared. Water should not be under- or over-boiled, as this will take away the chemical properties of the water and prevent the tea leaves from circulating in the best possible manner, the result being a weak, insipid brew. All teas which are not specifically described as quick brewing *must* be allowed to stand for at least three to four minutes. It is not fair to expect good results from a tea when all the different growths which make up the blend have not been given a chance to infuse properly. The blenders of the tea have chosen the teas so that they produce together a certain flavour. If the tea is poured out too soon and some of the teas are not infused, the flavour will be distorted.

The blending schedules completed, they are passed to the factory so that blending and packing can begin. The teas are put through a sifter and dust-extractor, being cut if necessary to make the leaf smaller, and from here fall into large drums, rotated a specific number of times in order to mix them thoroughly. The blended tea then passes over a magnet to extract any odd pieces of metal or nails which may have come from the chests, and on into bags for delivery to the automatic weighing and packing machines, remarkable for their speed and efficiency.

The tea is fed in at the top and falls under its own weight into the empty quarter-pound packs, the plunger forces the tea down into the packets; the ends are folded over, gummed and sealed. Most companies mark the packets with a code dating in the form of two indentations in the side of one of the labels. Any question about the tea can then be easily checked. Finally, the tea is sent to the retailer.

It is said that seven years are needed to train a tea taster, this time being spent buying Indian and Ceylon teas in London and other terminal markets abroad, and studying the art of blending. Perhaps the greatest factor which makes it such a long training is that it is only possible to note the seasonal variations in quality of each growth as and when they become available. At the end of this

training period one could certainly know how to buy and blend
teas, but it is always necessary to keep up with the newly developed
gardens and changes in style of manufacture, and there is always
more to learn.

A number of specialized branches of the trade are open to trained
tasters. Most become buyers or blenders for the blending and packing
companies. A smaller number, usually with family connections in
the firm, become selling brokers, valuing and auctioning, or buying
brokers advising on tea purchases. Agency houses managing the
gardens for producing companies need trained tasters with wide
experience, and there are also 'tea doctors' who visit tea factories
on the tea estates, making reports and advising on tea manufacture.
This is a particularly interesting and varied life.

There are only a hundred or so tea tasters in London now.
Many of them smoke and drink and I am sometimes asked if this
blurs the palate. I believe it does, though not sufficiently to detract
from the taster's ability to do his job. When tasters start training
it is better that they should not drink or smoke for a number of years
in order to safeguard and sharpen their palates, but once they are
sufficiently trained, with a knowledge of the various teas which they
are handling, smoking and drinking make little difference to the
skill, knowledge and experience they have acquired.

Early in 1968 I went back to Plantation House after an absence
of some years. I was with a business colleague who was interested to
see the auction room. I found it was closed and that the auctions
were being held in a temporary room, while a new auditorium,
smaller and more compact than the old one, was under construction.
It was a sign of the times, and by 1971 the auction room had moved
yet again. For years the attendances at the auctions have been gradually declining and the grand accommodation of the past is no longer
needed. Before the war there were about 200 firms dealing in tea
in Mincing Lane, now there are scarcely fifty.

This does not mean that the volume of trade is any less. On the
contrary, it is simply that the business has become steadily more
concentrated into fewer and larger companies. In tea, as in other
businesses, the tendency has been towards amalgamation. But I have
always been glad that I started in tea just soon enough to gain a
lasting impression of the Mincing Lane auctions in their more
expansive days.

Above, Fermented leaf being fed into firing machines for the drying process which changes the green tea into black tea. The made tea is taken from the bottom of the machines and spread on the floor to cool.

Left, Sifting machines grading the tea into leaf sizes, such as 'brokens', 'fannings' and 'dust'.

Tea chests being unloaded by automatic conveyor from Thames barges into Butlers Wharf below Tower Bridge.

Below, Customs officer supervising the drawing of samples from cases in a warehouse. Samples are taken from each chest and the hole is then filled with a metal bung.

Above, Tea brokers tasting samples of tea. They report on its quality to their clients, the company whose estate produced the tea, and also value the tea before it is put up for auction.

Assistant in a tasting room weighing each portion of tea in a balance.

Teas laid out for inspection. The tea is made in the pot and strained into the bowl through the holes made by the serrated edge of the pot and the lid. Milk is added to the tea and the leaf is displayed on the upturned lid.

A tea buyer and his assistant examining a batch from the hundreds of teas offered for sale each week at the London tea auctions.

The big auditorium in Plantation House, Mincing Lane; in use until the end of 1967.

A tea packing factory. The tea falls from hoppers on the top storey into packing machines below.

Tea bags being packed on a modern tea bag packing machine.

Above, At the sign of Pasqua Rosee's Head, the site of London's first coffee house in Change Alley, Cornhill. Sir Leslie Royce, Lord Mayor of London, unveiling a plaque to mark the tercentenary of its opening.

Left, Halfpenny token used by Pasqua Rosee.

The first coffee house which also sold tea. Garraway's coffee house in Change Alley just before it was demolished.

The interior of Garraway's coffee house in 1671. This was the original coffee house which started in a peruke-maker's shop and was burned down in 1748.

Above, The interior of Lloyd's coffee house, started by Edward Lloyd who published ship's lists and other maritime information and made his coffee house the cradle of modern marine insurance.

Left, The George Inn at Southwark, built in 1676. One of the few old coffee rooms still in existence.

3

The Rise and Fall of the Coffee House

At the beginning of 1952 I knew as little about coffee as I had about tea a few years before, but coming back home one evening after a day's tea-tasting I saw a small paragraph in the evening paper reporting that Sir Leslie Royce, then Lord Mayor of London, had unveiled a plaque to mark the tercentenary of the opening of London's first coffee house in Michael's Alley, Cornhill. A few days later I went along to have a look, and found the new plaque on the outside wall of the Jamaica Wine House, which had been a coffee house in the eighteenth century. Blue Mountain coffee from Jamaica is still served there.

The Jamaica Wine House stands on the site of the original London coffee house, opened in 1652 by Pasqua Rosee, and it was started, as seems to be the case with so many of the events that have had an important influence on English social history, almost by accident.

Although coffee has nearly as long a history as tea, it did not reach Europe until the seventeenth century. In England it was still a very novel beverage indeed when Daniel Edwards, a much travelled merchant who had trading connections with Turkey, brought supplies of coffee back with him to London. Finding that his house was seldom free from guests who wanted to try the new drink, he arranged for his servant Pasqua Rosee, whom he had brought from Turkey, to prepare and serve coffee to offer for sale to the public. Thus began a social revolution which swept all London; a revolution which was to repeat itself in the coffee-bar era just three centuries later.

I was aware that coffee had been established in England for about as long as tea, but the plaque on the wall of the Jamaica Wine House brought the fact home to me for the first time. The coffee market, since the decline of the eighteenth-century coffee houses, had been in the doldrums right up to the 1930's, but the Americans

D

who had been in England as soldiers during the war were beginning
to come back as tourists, and always it was coffee they wanted to
drink, rarely tea. I thought I could see signs that coffee was due for a
revival.

Ethiopia is believed to have been the original home of coffee about
the sixth century A.D. The Ethiopians discovered the sustaining
qualities of the wild coffee plant, and chewed the beans on their long
journeys across the deserts and mountains when they were forced
to travel light and could not depend on finding food along the way.
Arab slave raiders probably picked up the idea from them and took
it home. Evidence shows that coffee plants were first actually cultivated in the Yemen.

At that time two drinks were made from the berry. One was
prepared from the beans which were roasted and ground, first done
(it is believed) by the Persians, producing coffee more or less as
we know it. The other was a wine prepared by fermenting the soft
sweet pulp and cherry-skin of the berry. The origin of the word
coffee is obscure, though it is possibly derived from the Arabic
kahwah.

Although these are more or less accepted facts, there are several
picturesque legends which deal with the birth of coffee. Probably
the best known tells how over a thousand years ago an Arab goat-
herd was amazed to see that after his goats had eaten the leaves and
berries of a particular tree they became playful and frisky. He fetched
the abbot of the nearby monastery, who picked some of the berries,
steeped them in water, served the liquid to his lethargic monks,
and found to his satisfaction that they no longer fell alseep over their
prayers, but instead were reverent and attentive.

Coffee became a popular drink among the Moslems when
Mohammed decreed that those who drank wine should never enter
Paradise. It quickly spread to Aden and Medina, and the pilgrims
carried it with them to Mecca, but it did not reach Cairo and Syria
until the sixteenth century. From about 1554 traders brought coffee
from Aleppo and Damascus in Syria to Constantinople. A factor
which retarded its progress was the Arabs' reluctance to allow coffee
to be cultivated outside their own lands. For many years they refused
to allow coffee beans to leave the country unless they had been cooked
to prevent their use as seeds. Coffee became so popular in Constantinople that prayers were neglected, and the coffee houses brought
upon themselves the disfavour of the religious authorities in the
mosques.

At first, all commercial coffees came from the Yemen, where they
were shipped from the port of Mocha. The Yemen produces coffee

still, but shortly after the First World War the water wells at Mocha dried up and nearly all the commercial population had to leave. Nowadays coffee from the Yemen is exported from Hodeida, but the traditional name of Mocha is still used for Arabian coffees, as well as those from other countries which resemble it in colour and taste.

There is a popular song which says that 'there's an awful lot of coffee in Brazil', and it is quite possible that the great coffee industry of that country and indeed most of the coffee in South America, Central America and the West Indies, was started from a single coffee tree. King Louis XIV of France was presented in 1714 with a young, healthy plant by the Burgomaster of Amsterdam, and this was the progenitor. Two attempts were made to transport plants grown from the seed of this tree to the French colonies in the West Indies, but without success.

The credit for introducing coffee to the New World goes to a French Army officer named Mathieu des Clieux who set sail from Nantes in 1723 in a French merchantman, with three plants. After a voyage made eventful by storm, calm, corsairs, water shortage, and the machinations of a personal enemy who had designs on the precious plants, these ancestors of coffee in the Americas were triumphantly planted in Martinique.

Protected by thorn-bushes and a faithful band of slaves, the plants were surrounded in a few short years by a flourishing family of which even the Grand Monarch could have felt proud. All this resulted from 2 lb. of coffee seeds which des Clieux had gathered from the first harvest and given to his friends to plant. But another factor helped too. In 1721 tempests and an earthquake wiped out all the cocoa trees on which the local people depended for their livelihood. Cocoa was replaced by coffee, which soon multiplied to such an extent that cultivation spread to neighbouring islands and then to the mainland of South America.

*　　　*　　　*　　　*　　　*

Oxford lays claim not only to being the place where coffee was first drunk in England but also to possessing the first English coffee house. The former claim is substantiated by a reference in Evelyn's diary of 1637, where we learn of its being taken by a member of Balliol College. The coffee house, which was called the *Angel*, was opened thirteen years later by a Lebanese named Jacob. Dons and students found, as the Moslems had, that the new beverage acted as a stimulant, besides being pleasant to drink.

In 1652 Pasqua Rosee's first London coffee house, already mentioned, heralded a fashion that literally percolated into every street
and alleyway, and in so doing it greatly influenced the lives and
habits of the City merchants, particularly those in the neighbourhood
of the Royal Exchange, the centre of London commerce. Into the
coffee houses came men of many trades and callings to discuss their
deals and sales over a drink, knowing that the men they wished to
meet would be there. Some of the greatest of our modern commercial
institutions started life in a coffee house.

Towards the end of the seventeenth century the stockbrokers
deserted the Royal Exchange for the coffee houses, among them
Jonathan's and *Garraway's* in Change Alley off Cornhill. In 1773, as
the Government and trading enterprises began to raise money by
public subscription, they decided that they needed premises of
their own, which they found in Threadneedle Street. Visitors to
the public gallery of the Stock Exchange today can look down upon
the 'floor of the House', so named ever since the coffee-house days.
Similarly, the attendants are still called waiters, their blue and
red uniforms with gold-braided top hats standing out among the
members.

Another important institution which began in the coffee houses
is the Baltic. This mercantile shipping exchange, whose chief function
is the booking of cargoes in merchant vessels, was founded in its
modern form in 1903, following the amalgamation of the Baltic Club
with the London Shipping Exchange. Originally, business was done
at the *Virginia* and *Baltic* coffee houses, so called because the bulk
of the freight came from America and the Baltic countries.

Cargoes were auctioned in the saleroom provided on the premises,
and in the coffee room ships' captains and merchants were supplied
with newspapers and kept informed of trading developments. Later,
as business increased, the *Antwerp Tavern* in Threadneedle Street
was purchased and renamed the *Baltic*. On this same site the present
building stands, and as in the Stock Exchange, the attendants at
the Baltic are still called waiters.

Lloyd's, the most famous name in world insurance, started as a
coffee house. Policy brokers of the seventeenth century, seeking
subscribers, found the coffee houses invaluable. Instead of trailing
round from one office to another, they frequented certain of the
coffee houses where many of the men they were looking for could
be found at the same time.

One such coffee house was kept by Edward Lloyd, and it was
patronised by those business men most interested in marine insurance.
Lloyd's was originally situated in Tower Street, its address being

advertised in the *London Gazette* of 1688. Three years later *Lloyd's* moved to Lombard Street, next to the General Post Office, a convenient location, for by a private arrangement *Lloyd's* obtained the shipping lists from the Postmaster General.

After eighty years in Lombard Street the institution moved into Pope's Head Alley, subsequently into the Royal Exchange, Leadenhall Street, and finally into Lloyd's new building in Fenchurch Street, opened by Queen Elizabeth the Queen Mother in 1957. The focal point of this famous building is 'the room', in which more than 2,000 underwriters, brokers and their staffs may be seen at work. Here again, just as in the Stock Exchange and the Baltic, the uniformed attendants are known as waiters, a reminder of Edward Lloyd's original coffee house nearly 300 years ago.

*   *   *   *   *

After the strict regime of Oliver Cromwell there were many reasons for the popularity of the early coffee houses in addition to their usefulness as meeting places for merchants. The roasting and grinding of the coffee beans must have attracted considerable attention. In contrast to the taverns, the coffee houses offered not only good value and novelty but also an economical, non-alcoholic manner in which to spend a pleasant evening. Medical men seeking a cure for drunkenness hailed the arrival of coffee with enthusiasm; and certainly in the coffee houses there followed much sober but scintillating discussion. Men from all walks of life found pleasure in this new environment where they could mix freely and keep up with current affairs in the relaxation of tension which followed the Restoration.

But coffee houses did not have everything their own way. Other traders in the City complained bitterly of the new and (to them) obnoxious smell that came from the roasting of beans by night and day. Most alarmed, somewhat naturally because of the fire risk, were the booksellers. Alehouse keepers were loud in their complaints, fearing that their trade would decline from the new competition, and they encouraged such detrimental descriptions of coffee as 'syrup and soot' and 'essence of old shoes'.

Even the tragedy of the Great Plague of 1665 could not dampen the popularity of the coffee houses, although in those dangerous times a customer on arrival would be closely questioned concerning the health of his family. After the Great Fire of the following year the coffee houses were among the first buildings to reappear in the City. Their rapid growth, over the next fifty years, from the vicinity of the Royal Exchange and Fleet Street to Bishopsgate, Charing

Cross, the Strand, Southwark, the Barbican, Westminster down to St. James's provided ample proof of their necessity to the business community. They were also the kingpin on which the social life of the City revolved.

Nevertheless, the Government of the day regarded the growth of the coffee houses with concern and suspicion, and they found unexpected support from another section of society, the women. The wives of the men who frequented the coffee houses had already found much cause for complaint because they felt their menfolk were being lured away from them by a new-found freedom.

But their reasons for attacking coffee, expressed in 'The Women's Petition Against Coffee', were more subtle, yet more dangerous. They raised a spectre which had caused consternation in many countries from time to time for all sorts of curious reasons—a falling birth-rate. In down-to-earth terms which left no room for misunderstanding they accused coffee of making the men sterile and even impotent. It made them, so the women alleged, 'as unfruitful as the sandy deserts, from where that unhappy berry is said to be brought'.

They protested that the coffee houses provided a refuge in times of domestic crises when a husband should have been attending to his duties at home, and so they aroused sympathy at the same time as striking at the very root of their menfolk's self-respect.

Their manifesto was soon followed by a spirited counter-attack by the coffee-drinkers. This was 'The Men's Answer to the Women's Petition', and in similar fearless prose it sought to vindicate both coffee and those who drank it. It was a brave defence, but whatever effect it had on the women, its impression on the Government was disappointing.

King Charles II himself was moved to intervene. Using the women's grievances as an excuse, but in reality glad of a chance to put an end to all the undesirable forgathering, he issued a Royal Proclamation on December 29th, 1675, that all coffee houses should be closed within two weeks. The King hoped that this measure would put an end to too much talk and possibly sedition, for this was the time when he was trying to become independent of Parliament and to restore an absolute monarchy on the French model.

But such was the public outcry against this interference with the people's liberty that the Proclamation was rescinded, and the coffee houses remained open. In fact they remained open for a hundred years to come, the centre of London's social and business life.

Many coffee houses opened in London away from the area of the Royal Exchange, and although they were democratic places, it soon became clear that each art and profession preferred its own special coffee house, just as the traders in the City had.

Owing to the plague and the subsequent fire, coffee houses frequently moved to new sites, and moreover there was often more than one coffee house of the same name, making individual research difficult.

Bastons in Cornhill was patronised by medical men who met to discuss their profession, and also to attend patients who knew where to find them. Estate agents went to the *London* in Ludgate Hill, where property was auctioned by candlelight. *The George* in the Strand, near Temple Bar, was popular with barristers and lawyers, who no doubt met to sharpen their wits and conversation on one another. *The Chapter* in Paternoster Row was the rendezvous of booksellers, and here they bought copyrights from playrights and authors. It was well known that men of fashion, wealthy citizens, artists and foreigners all had their favourite coffee houses. Likewise the politicians: the Tories meeting at *Ozindas*, and the Whigs at *St. James*.

For the price of one penny (which indicated that the customer was willing to abide by the rules) the coffee house was open to any man who cared to go in. The atmosphere was smoke-laden, and in the more popular coffee houses groups stood so tightly packed together that it was hard to tell where one ended and another began— listening to the gems of wisdom which fell from the lips of the literary and political men of the moment. Here a man was safe from his womenfolk (who were forbidden to enter); and although the ladies in their drawing rooms complained about the situation, in truth no gentlewoman would have cared to set foot in the early coffee house.

Smoke from the big open fires mingled with the tobacco smoke from the clay pipes and the aroma of coffee constantly being roasted and brewed. The smell was strengthened by the scents used by the fops and by the perfumed pomades with which most men dressed their hair. Baths were not the institution they are today, and as most men rode on horseback, or at least drove, they carried the smells of the stable with them. Although this would have seemed unpleasant to modern noses, it passed almost unnoticed by the robust generations who lived in seventeenth-century London. As the evening wore on, the light shed by the oil lamps and candles fought a losing battle with the thickening atmosphere, so that it was no longer possible to read the broadsides, newspapers or Rules of the House thoughtfully provided by the proprietors.

Amid the hubbub, waiters and serving wenches squeezed their way to and fro to serve dishes of steaming coffee (at 2d. a time) to make for more good fellowship and inspire more talk. Often scandal and gossip were the main topics of conversation, and many reputations were made or broken. The more fortunate managed to find seats on the hard, high-backed chairs which flanked the long trestle tables of dark, heavy wood, while the famous had places reserved for them in their favourite corners, places where they could always be found and where their disciples knew they could join the court of the Master. Latecomers and strangers had often to make do with whatever standing room they could find. But if they failed to station themselves near enough to a wit or personality they could always depend on having his *bons mots* repeated to them by someone in the inner circle.

The coffee houses were responsible for giving us many of the accepted customs known today. In the *Turk's Head* the now-familiar ballot box first made its appearance. It was referred to by the members as 'our wooden oracle', and was used when discussions were settled by vote. The *Turk's Head*, appropriately enough, was in Westminster. The pernicious habit of tipping started when patrons of coffee houses, in order 'To Insure Promptness', placed money in a box marked T.I.P.

The invaluable shipping lists delivered daily to commercial firms originated as we know in Edward Lloyd's coffee house. Auctioning of commodities like coffee, tea and property began in the coffee houses where separate salerooms were provided.

Here, too, Steele and Addison gathered information of a different type for the *Spectator* and the *Tatler*. Not only did these literary gentlemen gather their copy from the coffee houses, they also relied on them for their circulation, and this convenient means of gleaning and distributing information soon had an astonishing and beneficial effect on manners and good taste. The good standing of the Press in the days of Steele and Addison can be attributed directly to the coffee houses, though in later years the coffee houses and the Press came into conflict.

The newly formed state postal service received a fillip when it became common practice to use coffee houses as accommodation addresses, and as receiving and distributing centres for overseas mail, most of which travelled by private ship. Coffee as a cure for all ills was also an early subject for the advertising copywriter.

As the latter half of the seventeenth century progressed, coffee-drinking spread to other parts of Britain and across the Channel to Paris and Berlin. By 1700 there were even coffee houses in Russia, home of the samovar and of a nation traditionally devoted to tea. Coffee also travelled across the Atlantic to the more advanced parts

London coffee house scene in the early eighteenth century. The pots of coffee are being kept hot before the blazing fire, and it is possible that at this time these pots were also used for making tea.

Green coffee beans being roasted in a long-handled ladle by Bedouin in North Africa. The beans are then ground with the mortar and pestle.

The Women's Petition Against Coffee.

THE
WOMEN'S
PETITION
AGAINST
COFFEE.

REPRESENTING
TO
PUBLICK CONSIDERATION
THE
Grand INCONVENIENCIES accruing
to their SEX from the Excessive
Use of that Drying, Enfeebling
LIQUOR.
Presented to the Right Honorable the
Keepers of the Liberty of *VENUS*.

By a Well-willer ————

London, Printed 1674.

The Men's Answer.

THE
Mens Answer
TO THE
Womens Petition
AGAINST
COFFEE:

VINDICATING
Their own Performances, and the Vertues of
their Liquor, from the Undeserved
Aspersions lately Cast upon
them, in their
SCANDALOUS PAMPHLET.

LONDON, Printed in the Year 1674.

A plaque opposite Queen's College, Oxford, which records the introduction of coffee to England.

NEARBY STOOD
THE ANGEL INN
WHERE ONE JACOB
OPENED

THE FIRST
COFFEE HOUSE
IN ENGLAND

IN THE YEAR

1650

Below, Map showing the location of many of the old London coffee houses before the fire of 1748.

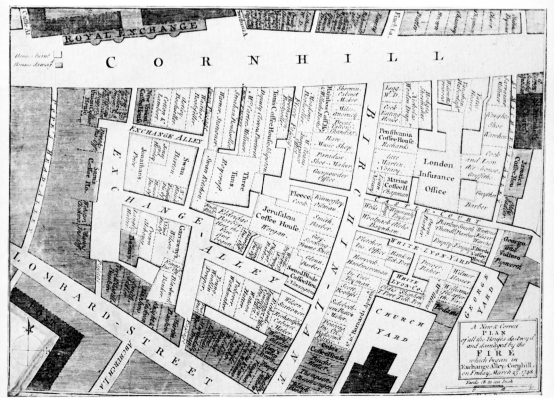

Above, Picking arabica coffee cherries on Kilimanjaro. In the background are the perpetual snows of Kibo crater.

Left, Coffee in flower on Kilimanjaro.

Opposite, Close-up of coffee cherries ready for picking.

Coffee in flower.

Plantation coffee laid out in rows near Kilimanjaro.

Pulping machine removing the outer skin from coffee cherries.

Above, Tanks in which the mucilage surrounding the coffee parchment is fermented to make it separate easily.

Left, Washing coffee after fermenting to remove the mucilage.

of the New World, but by this time its importance in Britain had
begun to decline.

Gradually the rules of the coffee houses which made them accepted meeting places for all sections of society and commerce fell into
disuse. Strong liquor found its way into the coffee houses, and although it was possible to sober up with coffee at the opposite end of
the bar to which alcohol was taken, snobbery reared its head,
particularly among the intelligentsia, who felt that their special
genius entitled them to protection from the common herd. Strangers
were no longer welcome.

Literary clubs sprang up which competed with the coffee houses,
and soon showed signs of outnumbering them. Men whose interests
leaned towards politics also banded together, the Whigs at the
Kit-Kat Club and the Tories at the Brothers Club, although there
were many other clubs formed for political purposes. It was a period
when party politics were becoming increasingly important, and the
frivolities of coffee-drinking were lost in more serious discussion.
At the same time, business men found that they could carry on their
commercial activities more conveniently in the more businesslike
surroundings of the special marketing institutions and associations,
or in their own offices, rather than in the coffee houses.

The coffee-house proprietors contributed to their own decline
through foolish over-confidence. Seeing the Press becoming more
and more influential, they tried to make the coffee houses the
exclusive source of news, and this met with strong resistance from
the public.

Two other sections of the community viewed these changes with
satisfaction and helped as much as they could to hasten the decline.
The Government was pleased to see that fashion had achieved what
the King himself had failed to do years before. The British East
India Company was importing more and more tea from the Far
East, and the Government was doing its best to foster the growing
trade. Tea became fashionable at Court, and the ladies in their
drawing rooms lent the movement every assistance both by drinking
tea at every opportunity and discouraging their men from going to
the coffee houses. In some respects, however, the ladies were less
successful than the Government; they encountered, instead, the
bogey of the clubs—and to this problem they have not to this day
found a solution!

There was a further reason for the decline. Ever since the Commonwealth, when many loyal Royalists had lost all they had, men
from aristocratic families had joined the bands of highwaymen and
footpads who infested the highways. To the highly born this was

something in the nature of a part-time job, because in their off-duty hours they went to the coffee houses with the more respectable members of the community, and there they often picked up much useful information of rich travellers. This brought many of the coffee houses into disrepute, and those who sought peace and security retired to the safety and privacy of their clubs.

The coffee houses had contributed a great deal to the social history of their time, and they saw the emergence of a new and influential class of men, men of moderate means, good education and modern ideas; men who learned that they could successfully oppose the will of the monarch, and even get rid of him and appoint a new one, that they could see the country governed according to their wishes, express their views freely in the Press, organize trade and revolutionize literature. These men needed meeting places and in the coffee houses they found them.

But the century of consolidation was over. The new giants of politics, such as Pitt and Fox, the merchant princes, the romantic poets of the early nineteenth century, all these would have found the atmosphere uncongenial. The coffee houses faded away.

Because tea is regarded as our national drink, it still seems surprising to many people that the British were once such heavy coffee-drinkers, though admittedly only for a short time at the height of the coffee-house era.

By 1886 consumption of coffee per head was down to 1·02 lb. and for tea it was up to 3·42 lb. The reasons for the trend are clear. To brew tea, all that is needed is to add boiling water; coffee, in contrast, requires roasting, grinding and brewing. In the latter part of the seventeenth century and the first half of the eighteenth this was done in the coffee houses, but the art could not be so easily carried out in the home.

British sea power also played its part. The swift clipper ships rushed tea here direct while coffee supplies from Africa and Asia were often held up in their journey by local wars and revolutions.

Tea consumption per head had increased to 8·51 lb. by 1921, while the figure for coffee was down to only 0·74 of a lb. Not only had the coffee houses died, the taste for coffee had almost died too.

It seemed that the only way to persuade the British public to drink more coffee was to prepare it in a simpler form for brewing. The alternatives were a concentrated liquid essence, or a soluble dried-coffee extract in powder form. In the 1890's America took the initiative with a soluble dried-coffee extract which had three advantages: never-varying taste, quickness of preparation, and complete absence of grounds. In those days coffee enthusiasts said as they do today that a soluble powdered coffee could not compare for flavour with ground coffee properly prepared. Nevertheless, the idea was there, and progress could not be shackled.

A Japanese chemist from Tokyo, who had failed to market a soluble tea, turned to coffee in 1899. A company was formed, and the members of the Ziegler Arctic Expedition, who were among the first to use soluble coffee, found it satisfactory. Many other firms started manufacture, and during the First World War soluble coffee really came into its own when it was shipped in large quantities to the American forces serving in Europe.

At about this time Dr. Ludwig Roselius, anxious no doubt to overcome the idea that it is difficult to sleep after drinking coffee, discovered how to remove the caffeine. Such decaffeinated coffee is prepared from green beans, softened by steam, extracted with low boiling chlorinated solvents, then steamed again to remove residual solvent and dried. A popular blend currently being sold is the well known H.A.G. brand.

Meanwhile, in this country, the firm of R. Paterson and Son of Glasgow introduced the famous Camp liquid coffee essence towards the end of the nineteenth century. In its familiar tall square bottle, with a label picturing a kilted Scotsman outside his tent in some far outpost of the Empire, the essence quickly established itself. Its popularity was confirmed in both world wars, when sales were sacrificed to maintain quality while coffee was scarce. It is remarkable that despite the success of instant coffee, output of Camp trebled between 1939 and the early 1950's.

In 1938 Nestlés first introduced Nescafé on the Continent, and a year later it came to Britain. Its story is one of the biggest post-war marketing successes in this country.

To make a spray-dried coffee, the beans required for the blending schedule are mixed in a rotating drum, then roasted, cooled and ground. The coffee then goes into giant percolators standing three storeys high—producing the equivalent of thousands of household coffee-pots in almost the same way that coffee is made at home. In these huge percolators hot water is pumped through under such pressure that practically none of the flavour is lost, and with the aid of delicate instruments the proper degree of percolation is carefully controlled. The liquid is then turned into powder in a stainless-steel dryer.

It is the importation of coffee for making spray-dried coffee, which is, of course, manufactured by several other firms as well as Nestlés, that is largely the reason for the rise in coffee imports over the last few years, and the increase in consumption from 0·88 lb. per head in 1939 to the present 3½ lb. Another reason was the mushroom growth of coffee bars.

In the post-war years there were one or two coffee rooms in London and elsewhere, but none was of great significance. Then on 17th July 1952 a group of people from occupations as far apart as farming and the Civil Service opened a contemporary *Coffee House* at 3 Northumberland Avenue, Trafalgar Square. The object was to provide a meeting place in pleasant surroundings with an informal atmosphere where good coffee (prepared by the percolator method) and other refreshments could be served at modest prices.

In a modern setting it followed the tradition of London's early coffee houses 300 years before. To encourage young, up-and-coming artists, it was decided to give wall-space for monthly exhibitions of paintings, and by the beginning of 1960 nearly a hundred had been given. The *Coffee House* of Northumberland Avenue proved an interesting and successful experiment, but one which was not widely repeated. The reason was not far to seek. Only a month after the *Coffee House* opened its doors, London heard for the first time the sizzling espresso machine in the pioneer coffee bars, and it was with these that the future lay.

Having studied the development of the coffee business so far, I started to investigate the origin of the espresso machine, the first attempt at automatic coffee-making, but before I could fully understand this it seemed to me that I must first get some practical experience of coffee-tasting. I heard from a friend that there was a job going with a firm which acted as brokers to the Kenya Coffee Board in Nairobi, so I arranged to meet a representative of the company who was then in London. An appointment was made at Walsingham House, Seething Lane, and here I met a director of Kenya Coffee Auctions who told me that the company wished to increase its staff in East Africa. I was eager to join. In due course I was offered the job, though since I had no practical experience of coffee in any of its aspects it could only have been my enthusiasm to learn that got it for me.

I think some of my friends and colleagues at Lyons thought I was being foolish in the extreme to turn in a good job with sound prospects and security and go off to unsettled conditions in East Africa, but they wished me well in my new venture. I packed and set off for Africa once again.

4

Coffee Break in East Africa

The arabica coffees of Kenya and Tanzania are among the best in the world, yet coffee was late in coming to East Africa. Although Abyssinia and Arabia, the original home of coffee, are almost next door, the first Arabian coffee was brought from the island of Réunion, near Mauritius, by Roman Catholic missionaries in about 1893. The Catholic Fathers had similarly played a major part in introducing coffee-growing to South America more than a hundred years before. German settlers planted seed, obtained from the mission stations, on the slopes of Kilimanjaro and Meru in what was then German East Africa, and soon afterwards a robusta coffee was tried west of Lake Victoria, where it was grown for export by the Bukoba tribe.

Coffee is an evergreen, so it does not need a great deal of rain, but it does need sub-soil moisture all the year round, the arabica strains thriving better in cool but frost-free areas and the robusta strains growing satisfactorily in more typically tropical temperatures. All over the world volcanic soil is the kind that coffee likes best. It does not like wind. The type of soil, rainfall, acidity of soil, temperature and altitude which coffee will tolerate all had to be discovered by trial and error. In the Usambara Mountains and Nyasaland the plants would bear such good crops in their first year or two that they became exhausted and an easy prey to disease and pests. Fortunately, in East Africa there was practically no fear of the frosts which occasionally cause severe damage in the coffee-growing areas of Brazil.

The Germans on Kilimanjaro had an almost complete grasp of the many and varied needs of the coffee plant, but they made one error which was to become extremely costly. The German Government appropriated the lower land on the south-eastern slopes of Kilimanjaro and Meru for the German plantations and left the upper, cooler, mistier slopes to the Chagga tribes. In fact it was the upper slopes which proved to be the best coffee land and which have made the Chagga one of the richest tribes in Africa.

The 1914–18 war cleared the German planters from German East Africa, which was then handed over to Great Britain to be administered as a Mandated Territory. The old German estates were sold very cheaply, mostly to Greeks and Indians who made a good deal of money from them. These were to be the only freehold property in the new Tanganyika Territory which henceforth was held in trust for the native population only and was not available to European settlers.

In the first years of the century Kenya was a very poorly developed country with virtually no roads. A few Europeans with little experience of coffee experimented with seed obtained from the French Fathers at the Roman Catholic Mission in Nairobi, usually setting aside a little piece of land for it on their mixed farms so that a failure would not be too disastrous. When coffee production began to form an important part of Kenya's economy the Government started intensive research which brought about great improvements in methods of cultivation and pest control. Coffee-growing in Kenya quickly developed into one of the finest managed coffee industries in the world.

Before and just after the last war Kenya had great appeal for the British. It has a marvellous climate, splendid scenery and the best big-game hunting in the world, and it also had the highest proportion of ex-army officers and 'younger sons' of all the British colonies. The settlers had a great reputation for enjoying themselves, even many years after the early days of the colony when it had been described as 'a place in the sun for shady people', and Kenyans, being mostly independent-minded, did not allow themselves to be troubled overmuch by the Colonial Office. The settlers were very hard-working people and put in long hours to make their farms prosperous, often in areas which were so unknown and untried that there was no means of telling which crops would grow or whether animals could survive. They loved Kenya and regarded themselves as real Kenyans, there to stay for ever, until their peace was rudely shattered in the early 1950's by the Mau Mau troubles. Kenya was never really the same again.

In the immediate post-war period the coffee market in East Africa was under the control of the Ministry of Food, but as things returned to normal, and food rationing in Britain was abolished, this came to an end and the coffee growers and the coffee trade made their own arrangements to market coffee. Since coffee was grown in several ways—by independent farmers, both settlers and Africans;

by co-operatives and under schemes sponsored by the various colonial governments—selling arrangements were flexible and were adapted to suit the different areas. Kenya, Uganda and Tanganyika were at this time a federation, and although Uganda robusta coffee was sold in a way peculiarly its own, and which will be described later, Kenya and Tanganyika's arabica industries were much more closely associated and there was a constant interchange of ideas, particularly as the firms of coffee brokers had branches in each important coffee-growing area of the federation and frontiers were of little significance.

Many of the companies engaged in the coffee trade had their offices in Etco House in Nairobi, which also housed the coffee-auction room. The auctions in Kenya and Tanganyika were organized and run on behalf of the colonial governments by Kenya Coffee Auctions, the firm for which I was to work, which also traded on its own behalf as coffee brokers. After independence, arrangements for marketing coffee became part of the responsibility of state-sponsored coffee boards.

When I arrived in Nairobi in 1954 it was a rapidly expanding city. There was a new Princess Elizabeth Highway and new roads to other parts of the colony had brought it very much up to date and out of the era of native bearers, but my stay in Kenya was short. My employers were anxious to send me as soon as possible to Moshi in Tanganyika, since if I stayed in Nairobi I might be conscripted into the police because of the Mau Mau emergency. There was only time for me to meet one or two buyers and visit the Nairobi coffee-grading mill, a fascinating experience, since it was my first sight of vast quantities of coffee. I also briefly met the liquorer to the Coffee Board of Kenya to taste some coffee, which we did without milk. It did not at first have the same appeal as tea-tasting, but I anticipated no difficulty in adjusting my palate and expected to find coffee as absorbing as tea.

The manager of the Moshi office of Kenya Coffee Auctions was W. Robert Forder, now adviser to the Ethiopian Coffee Board, and he was good enough to come up to Nairobi by car to collect me. The drive south on the Great North Road into Tanganyika and on to Moshi at the foot of Mount Kilimanjaro is only 200 miles, but the first part from Nairobi to the border was rough with many pot-holes and ran through undulating scrub dotted with giraffe and wilde-beest. From the Tanganyika border the road was metalled and a joy to drive on, and the scrubland gave way to European-owned farms as we neared Arusha. By-passing Arusha, the road curls round the lower slopes of Mount Meru, a considerable mountain of 17,000 feet

with the crater of an extinct volcano at the top, and on through the
Masai Plain, which is a huge area of 20,000 square miles inhabited
exclusively by the Masai, one of the greatest tribes in Africa. The
40,000 Masai, a cattle-owning and aritsocratic people, have always
refused to adopt the European's way of life and do not like education.
They are much admired for their beautiful physique and picturesque
clothes and ornaments, but now that they are no longer allowed to
go cattle-raiding or harry the neighbouring tribes there is little for
their young warriors to do except start minor feuds and be studied
by film-camera units and anthropologists. They still try to prove
their manhood by killing a charging lion with a spear.

Moshi, I found, was a prosperous, cosmopolitan little town.
Before World War II it had been something of a Nazi stronghold,
the old German planters had been replaced by a new generation
fresh out from the Fatherland, but now the Germans had gone for
the second time, leaving an assortment of British, Greeks, Italians,
Africans and Indians. There was the Kilimanjaro Hotel, the Moshi
Club, a pretty, white-painted Greek church, and the District Commissioner's office. There seemed to be no racial tension whatever.
It was undoubtedly coffee that was responsible for much of the new-
found wealth of the town, and coffee was grown up above us on the
slopes of Kilimanjaro, mostly in the territory of the Wachagga.

If the Masai are one of the bravest tribes of Africa, the Chagga
are probably the most intelligent. The Germans had put them in
possession of the best coffee-growing areas on the mountain, although
at the time the Chagga would have preferred the lower slopes,
where they could have grazed their cattle. Within a few years they
realized their luck, as they started gowing coffee in a haphazard
way on their own. Hopeful Europeans realized it too, and did their
best to get the land for themselves. However, the local Colonial
Administrators, in particular Sir Charles Dundas, the Secretary for
Native Affairs, held fast and insisted that the mandate from the League
of Nations should be unswervingly carried out. 'On the mountain
masses of Kilimanjaro and Meru and in certain parts of the Mbulu
district, the native possesses a natural heritage unequalled anywhere
in Africa', they said, and the Chagga kept their land.

The Chagga are expert iron and steel workers and could build
good roads and irrigation channels, but they had no gift for organization and were among the most quarrelsome people in Africa.
There are many deep gorges on Kilimanjaro in which the chiefs
could gather their people and carry on their feuds with the people
of the next gorge for whole generations. Something had to be done
to bring the tribe together to grow and sell their coffee in the most

efficient and economical way possible. The Chagga were gradually persuaded to elect a paramount chief over the approximately thirty independent chiefs they had before, and a European manager was appointed to advise them on cultivation, irrigation, processing and marketing. By 1953–4 their crop yielded 6,000 tons, worth about three and a half million pounds.

In addition the Chagga built their own hospitals and schools, and their prosperity contributed a lot to that of the European planters, since together they commanded an impressive place for their coffee in the overseas markets. The Kilimanjaro Native Co-operative Union and the Europeans became partners in the running of a coffee-curing factory. The Chagga set the example for many other native co-operatives in East Africa and in particular a similar one on Meru Mountain, where the Wa-Arusha tribe also plant coffee in affiliation with the Kilimanjaro Association.

From west to east over the gorges that slope down from the 13,000-foot saddle joining Kibo and Mawenzi (the two peaks of Kilimanjaro) the native planters belonged to over thirty individual societies affiliated to the Kilimanjaro Native Co-operative Union. Forder explained that the individual members of each society picked and processed their coffee cherries, delivering them in what is called 'parchment form' to their local co-operative stores where they received a nominal payment on each delivery. Dependent on the quality of the parchment, it was divided into two standards, special and ordinary, and stored separately.

When sufficient parchment was available to make up a delivery it was transported by lorry to the Moshi Mill where each delivery was milled, and the two green coffee beans from each cherry were graded for size and weight. Samples were tasted and each grade classified by a numbering system, 1 being the best and 13 the most inferior. It was then possible to issue bulking instructions so that the same grades of coffee with the same classification number could be bulked together in quantities suitable for sale.

A classification system of this sort ensures that inferior coffees are not allowed to detract from the better qualities and are most appropriate for the buyers' requirements. The Chagga growers received their outstanding payment through their own co-operative on the basis of the quality classification given by the coffee liquorer, as tasters are called in the coffee world, and the weight of coffee, and the payments made for each, were calculated at the end of the season when all the coffee had been sold.

Other coffee growers sent their coffee to Moshi to be valued and bulked in the same manner as the K.N.C.U. Since the growers have

E

not the knowledge or experience to be able to grade and judge their own coffee, they need an expert to do it for them and Kenya Coffee Auctions, as selling brokers for the K.N.C.U., did this. This procedure gave the coffee grower and his broker a much closer day-to-day relationship than that between the tea planter and his broker in London.

While I was receiving the basic instruction I was given a cup of locally grown tea which had an oil contamination and was not improved by the pondy-tasting water with which it was made. It also had watery milk and the off-white, locally grown sugar, containing hairs from the bags made from locally grown sisal in which it had been packed. Of all the horrible teas I ever tasted, this was the worst. Tanganyika tea is grown near the coast, where the Usambara Mountains catch the rain from the south-east monsoon. It is a similar quality to tea from Mlanje, quite pleasant if properly prepared, in fact modern tea from Tanzania has a high reputation.

In the next few days, as I tasted coffees, I realised that it would be easier for me to grasp how reports were made on the merits of each if I had a better understanding of how the K.N.C.U. arabica coffee was grown and processed. Accordingly, I made a little expedition up the mountain into Chaggaland. The Chagga live at about 4,000 feet in the belt of rain forest. The shambas, or smallholdings, are usually not much more than an acre or so and they are tucked into clearings in the forest, each shamba with its beehive hut, banana grove and vegetable patch and the coffee bushes, laid out in neat, dark green rows.

New tea is often raised from cuttings, but coffee, at least until recently, has nearly always been raised from seed. It takes a year for coffee seeds to become seedlings about twelve to eighteen inches in height, when they are planted eight to twelve feet apart, allowing plenty of room for growth. The tree yields its first crop in three to four years, but does not reach full maturity until the sixth year. Every year the trees are pruned and the soil is guarded against disease and pests.

The usual height of a coffee tree is between five and six feet, but if left unpruned it would grow, like the tea bush, as high as thirty feet and be quite useless. An average tree produces from 1 lb. to 4 lb. of coffee each year, and when the crop is good a man can pick in one day about 200 lb. of cherries, yielding up to 30 lb. of clean coffee.

When they are in blossom the trees are a sea of white with scented bloom like an English orchard. After the blossom has fallen the clusters of green cherries ripen to a deep red. The cherries each contain two beans, rounded one side and flat on the other, with the flat sides together. The beans are covered by a silver skin and encased by a husk, known as 'parchment'; this is surrounded by a sweet, gelatinous pulp, and, finally, there is the outer skin.

After the cherries have been picked they are taken to a processing unit where they are fed in a considerable flow of water into cylindrical pulping machines. Here serrated protrusions on a drum tear off the outer skins which are floated off along separate channels. The water is then drained away and the layer of mucilage surrounding the parchment is allowed to ferment for anything up to thirty-six hours. If, after this time, it comes away, leaving the parchment crisp and clean, it is ready for washing away. The coffee is then transferred to a final washing and grading channel, usually of concrete, two or three feet wide, about two feet deep and anything up to fifteen yards in length. At various points dams are fitted into grooves with the first part of the channel holding all the coffee in a considerable volume of water. Squeegees are used to push the coffee back against the water flow and any hollow beans, shells or skins, known as 'lights', rise to the top.

After the heavy coffee is partially clean and settled on the bottom, part of the first dam is removed, allowing the lights to run into the second section of the channel. After additional agitation of the coffee by squeegees, a further part of the first dam and part of the second are removed, allowing the lights to pass into the third section, the second-quality coffee passing into the second section. The water is drained off and the dams removed, leaving a long line of coffee in clean, sparkling parchment, separated into first and second quality.

The lights are disposed of and the coffee is placed on drying tables of hessian or wire mesh for drying in the open, taking anything from four days to a month, depending on the weather, to become thoroughly dry. During this stage the beans have to be turned constantly to ensure that they dry evenly. When properly dried the parchment around the two beans will come away if rubbed in the hand, exposing the solid beans, and in this condition the individual planters take the coffee to the society godowns.

It is not practicable to market coffee in parchment, as buyers would not be able to judge the overall quality of a lot, and if the beans vary in size some may be unsuitable for their requirements. So when a sufficient quantity is available it is transported to the Moshi Mill, where it is passed into hullers on the ground floor, the parchment being removed by a severe rubbing action; the beans and the parchment, now separated, fall through a rising air stream, the parchment being sucked out of the machine and the beans falling to an elevator which takes them to a grading rotary screen divided into sections, each having perforations of different sizes.

The beans are fed in at one end and gradually work down the spiral, finding their own particular outlet. The heavy, solid beans are graded A, B and C; A being the largest and C the smallest, though some producing countries use numbers instead of letters, describing the beans as first, second and third flats, the 'flat' referring to the flat side of the bean. After this, beans of similar size are graded for weight in air separating machines known as 'catadors', thus giving further grades, such as almost round beans known as 'peaberries' and beans above average size known as 'elephants'. 'Triage' or lowest-quality grades are also separated by the air blast, while the heavier defective beans are removed by hand. An approximate percentage of each grade would be: A 50, B 20, C 10, peaberries 4, elephants 3, triage 13.

Having acquired a better understanding of the way arabica coffee is processed and graded, I knew what to look for when tasting. In addition to detecting the inherent qualities sought after by buyers, and variations in quality due to climatic conditions, I was soon able to see faults in preparation: whether, for instance, the coffee had been picked too green, overripe, or after it had fallen to the ground; if the water used for pulping and washing was clean, or perhaps drawn in a beer barrel giving a flavour, and whether fermented in clean or dirty vats and for the right length of time. It is remarkable that all this can be determined by inspection and tasting without having seen the coffee cultivated and prepared, and that it is not possible for the grower to hide any defects. It is extremely important, therefore, especially to a co-operative group of growers where bulking has often to be done, that defects in preparation should be kept to a minimum.

As in tea-tasting, coffee liquorers deal with three major considerations when making their reports: the raw bean, corresponding to the dry leaf; the roasted bean, equivalent to the infused leaf; and the liquor obtained, in the case of coffee, from the roasted and ground bean, and each is divided again three times so that a greater degree of accuracy may be reached. The size of the raw bean may be very bold, bold, medium, mixed or small, the colour bluish, greyish blue, greyish green, greenish, greyish, brownish, brown or pale, while there may be a great number of defectives, an average number or none at all.

The roast is reported on according to colour; it may be brilliant, bright, ordinary or dull, while the centre cut, that is the line drawn down the centre of the flat side of each bean, may be white or brownish and the degree of actual roast of the bean very even, medium, or uneven, depending mainly upon the moisture content and quality.

The liquor is considered for acidity, body and flavour. The acidity may be pointed, medium, light or lacking; the body full, medium, light, lacking or harsh; the flavour fine, good, fair or poor.

After bulking has been completed, lists of all grades available for sale are printed in catalogues ready for the auction. These days the issuing of bulking instructions and organization of the auction is carried out by the Tanganyika Coffee Board, which retains in its title the old name of the territory, although the new independent state is called Tanzania. Before the auctions, which are held in Moshi every week during the season, samples are displayed locally and despatched to overseas buyers to enable them to submit orders to local buying agents. The Board value each grade according to quality and the ruling world coffee prices and also set a reserve price. After the auction buyers are invoiced and in the case of the K.N.C.U. the proceeds are distributed to the individual member societies in amounts calculated to be in accordance with the merits of their coffee as classified by the liquorer. For many years a substantial proportion of the money was retained in the tribal treasury and was used to build hospitals and schools and provide social services for the Chagga tribe.

I found the variations in colour of the green beans and their size gradings most interesting, but at first my work in the tasting room was not too enjoyable because of the strong smell of the beans being roasted and ground in large quantities, which was inclined to make me feel slightly sick. This was upsetting, because I had always liked, and still do, the heavy aroma of coffee being roasted in coffee shops in England. It was certainly contrary to my experience of a tea factory, which has a very pleasant smell while the tea is being manufactured.

While roasting cannot improve the quality of the beans, correct roasting is as important as any stage in the preparation—perhaps more so, for faulty roasting can have serious results. The sign of a good roast is for the beans to have an even chestnut colour, and not to be black and glistening with the essential and precious oils drawn to the surface, rapidly dissipating into the air. In a good roast the oils of the coffee will be retained in the beans and to an extent preserved by the hardened outside shell, so being stored ready to be released when the coffee is ground.

In the high roast, like that preferred on the Continent, the coffee is roasted until it is nearly black. The French sugar roast has sugar added which caramelizes with the heat and makes a shiny black bean. The accepted English roast is the stage when the beans are roasted nearly right through to the centre and when the porous cells containing the essential oils are so cooked that they will readily transfer their flavour and smell to the hot water when it is added. Rapid cooling is necessary after roasting, as it helps conserve the aroma of the coffee by closing up the pores of the bean.

As the season got under way, the days and weeks passed quickly with increased work, our job in the office being to taste and issue bulking instructions. Work began at eight o'clock with lunch from twelve-thirty until two, the office closing at four-thirty. Since dusk fell between six and seven it did not leave much daylight for social activities.

For Europeans these centred on the Moshi Club, and since there was a sizable European population, rugby football, soccer, cricket and tennis were all played in season, although we were almost on the Equator and there was no winter in the English sense, but rather a wet rainy season and a cool season. The new Moshi sports ground, overlooked by the glaciers of the Kibo Crater, must have one of the most spectacular settings in the world. The club side occasionally visited the main towns in the territory to play cricket matches, and I went with them to the coast to Tanga and also to Arusha, which is the starting point for safaris.

In the cool season, out of the main coffee-bearing time of the year, I took my local leave. It was the season when Kilimanjaro is comparatively clear of cloud and an ascent is possible. I met a South African from Johannesburg and a Scotsman from Nairobi who were as keen as I was to climb it. Kilimanjaro is the highest mountain in Africa, and when two German explorers returned from Africa in the middle of the nineteenth century, and said that there were mountains on the Equator with snow on their peaks, no one would believe them. Several attempts were made on Kilimanjaro by English and German climbers, but Dr. Hans Meyer, a famous Alpinist from Leipzig, was the first man to climb it in 1889 and found at the summit a glacier and the huge, snow-covered crater of Kibo, an extinct volcano. From 1933 onwards there have been signs of activity in the crater, though of a mild and not very spectacular type, and climbers reaching the top are urged by the Department of Geological Survey at Dodoma to go to the Ash Pit and see if they can see anything of interest. Although the regular route to the top of Kilimanjaro is not technically difficult, since it avoids major ice cliffs, it is a real test of stamina and fitness and many climbers are defeated by the altitude, which is not far short of 20,000 feet, combined with the cold, which above the rain forest is quite severe.

We started from the Kibo Hotel with our studded boots, warm clothing, food and blankets, and climbed for three days with the help of a Chagga guide and eight porters, spending the nights in climbers' huts *en route*. On the fourth day at two-thirty in the morning we left our porters at the Kibo hut at 16,000 feet and went on with the guide to complete the climb. We made the Kaiser Wilhelm-spitze at 19,340 feet, so overcome by exhaustion and altitude sickness that we barely had the strength to take a few photographs and sign our names in the book which is kept in a little tin trunk at the summit, with the bibles and national flags of climbers who have been there before. It had taken two and a half hours to complete the last mile and a quarter round the crater's rim. On the way down, the porters, who were as pleased at our success as we were, made us wreaths of red, pink and white everlasting flowers that conquerors of Kiliman-jaro are presented with to wear round their hats.

I had only been back a few days after our climb when I heard that I was to be transferred to the Company's Mombasa office, to give me the chance to learn about robusta coffee grown in Uganda but marketed and shipped from Mombasa.

Before leaving Moshi I visited the Coffee Experimental and Research Station at Lyamungo on the slopes of Kilimanjaro. I saw coffee being processed there on larger processing plant than that used by the Wachagga on their smallholdings. I discussed with a research officer the differences between the K.N.C.U. and similar East African arabica coffees and other world growths. In the Moshi office I had only seen local coffees and was therefore unable to observe the different liquoring characteristics, but from what I learnt then, and subsequently in London, I found that basically there are three main types of coffee produced in the world, known as mild, Brazilian and robusta.

The milds include all growths from the Central American continent, that is Guatemala, Salvador, Costa Rica, Venezuela, etc., the beans being bold, even and probably either bluish or greenish in colour. They are washed beans and the liquors have an acidity with plenty of life. Also in this group are the arabica coffees grown mainly in Africa—Kenya, Tanzania and the Congo—having bold, good-looking beans with even more acidity in the liquor than the Mexican and Colombian, though with a greater degree of harshness than the other milds, making this coffee very slightly less preferable to the British buyers than Central American, Mexican and Colombian coffees.

Coffee from Brazil, the largest producer in the world, has a more neutral character than the milds and there are a variety of qualities. The beans are smaller and more uneven than the mild types, with a percentage of black defectives, the number in any one parcel forming the basis of grading. The coffees take their description from the ports through which they are shipped, Santos, Parana, Rio or Victoria, and are graded according to the percentage of defectives, for instance a particular coffee may be described as 'Santos 2'. Coffees shipped from Rio and Victoria are usually regarded as more common in quality than those from Santos and Parana and sell at a discount over the corresponding grades.

The robusta coffee grows mainly in Africa and Asia and there are two types—natural, being unwashed, and washed. The natural is the poorest quality of all coffees with a thick, coarse liquor, often having a crude taste. Some robusta-producing countries, such as Uganda and Indonesia, have both washed and unwashed types and usually, as with the Brazilians, the defective and black beans in any one parcel form the basis of grading.

Broadly speaking, however, the milds are the most exclusive quality component of a blend giving quality, flavour and life. Brazilian coffees serve the purpose of supplying the bulk of the blend, and the more neutral-tasting robusta is added in proportions designed to retain a consistent retail selling price without damaging the quality of the blend. A possible ratio of each type of coffee in a blend would be five parts mild and arabica, four parts Brazilian and three parts robusta. Robusta coffee often gives a better 'extract rate' than Arabica coffee in soluble processing.

Coffee is usually blended for retail and restaurant sales in much the same way as tea, and each of the various growths or types have different values. In the United Kingdom the basic essentials that the coffee buyer and blender look for are acidity, body and flavour; the coffee must not be sourish or thin.

In more detail, the buyer notes the size, condition and hardness of the raw beans. A premium is often paid for a large size, though frequently the second size may have the better quality, but not so the third size, for this may include immature and defective beans. By turning over the beans in a tray or in the hand it is possible to note the evenness of colour, the number of defectives and also an occasional bean is cut open to note whether it is hard, waxy and tight inside.

Uganda-grown robusta coffee is mostly produced on small shambas, anything up to thirty acres in size, and the growing is left mostly to the women while the men work in the towns. Like much of the world's coffee it is prepared by the natural or dry method, the only possible method where water is scarce. The cherries, when ripe, are stripped by shaking them from the tree and laid on trays supported on stands until thoroughly dry, when they are called 'kiboko'. They are then taken in sacks to the nearest primary market where a co-operative mill removes the dried cherry skins, called husk, by threshing or in hulling machines. The coffee can then be washed in machines like domestic washing machines and afterwards dried by hot air.

Both unwashed and washed coffee is sold on type description. The Uganda Coffee Board issues grading certificates and, for this reason, once the taste of the main grades has been established, soon after the beginning of the season, it is not necessary, as with the arabica coffees, to taste each individual sample, and much of the Uganda robusta coffee with certified grades is bought without tasting—the business, as it were, being done on paper.

When I was in Africa the brokers in Nairobi and Moshi were mostly concerned with the sale of arabica coffee, while those in Kampala and Mombasa dealt with the robusta market. Their job was to encourage the sale, either by auction or private treaty, to the various East African traders and exporters in Nairobi and Mombasa who act as buying agents for European and American concerns. This was a local and rather simple form of 'futures' market. Business could be exciting when there were violent fluctuations in the market, brought about when exporters, in order to fulfil shipment dates and unable to obtain supplies from the producers, had to make purchases at increased prices from other shippers who held stocks. Nowadays the London Terminal market operates a vastly more sophisticated futures market to help protect the growers from disastrously low prices.

Mombasa is an old town by African standards and crammed with people of all nationalities. There is a large Arab population and the old port harbour is full of dhows which trade between the East African coast and Arabia, Persia and India with cargoes of copra, firewood, hides, mango poles and coconuts. And as usual in Africa, wherever there is trade there are many Indians.

Whenever I could I would get out of the office, which was nothing but paper work and ringing telephones, and take samples of coffee down to the old quarter and deal with the Arab and Indian shippers personally. They were always happy to be visited and we would discuss the market over endless cups of Turkish coffee or bottles of chilled orange squash. This hospitality was a great feature of doing business in the bazaars, and I enjoyed it much more than the transactions in the office, where my work gave me no opportunity to do any coffee liquoring, which seemed to me at the time the most interesting part of the coffee business.

After a few months I was not only missing the experience of tasting coffee but I also began to wonder whether my ability to taste tea was going to be wasted too. I considered my prospects in Africa in the light of the changes which the independence of the East African territories would inevitably bring about, and I decided to return to the tea trade in London.

5

The Boom in Coffee Bars

I soon found that while I had been away in Africa the boom in coffee bars had grown beyond all my expectations, and the fashionable new espresso machine was becoming well established.

Not that the espresso machines were really as new as all that, even in 1954. They were used in Italy well before the war, but the basic principles employed then were different from the post-war machines. Originally, steam was injected through the coffee, but the results were hardly satisfactory. Achille Gaggia became absorbed in the subject, and although his experiments were interrupted by the war, he designed and in 1946 marketed in Italy the first espresso to 'work without steam'. There may be a few of the early models still in use in this country bearing these words.

How did they work? The chrome-and-gold finish on the front and sides of these machines, seen all over Europe, covers a specially plated heavy-copper pressure boiler which rests on the counter-top. Inside the water is heated to boiling point and controlled automatically at a pressure of 20 lb. per square inch. Fixed to the tank are cylinders containing pistons worked by powerful springs. A filter holder containing the coffee is clamped to the bottom of each cylinder. On top is a lever, rather like a beer pump, which controls the piston. When the lever is pulled down, water drawn from the bottom of the boiler (to exclude steam) flows on to the coffee. When the lever is released the spring drives the piston downwards, forcing the water through the coffee at a pressure of about 60 lb. per square inch, ensuring that all the properties of the coffee are extracted, plus a few that no doubt the blender and roaster had intended should be left behind.

In Italy Gaggia's new principle was quickly recognized as revolutionary and his machines were soon selling through most of Europe as fast as the factory in Milan could turn them out, but the story of how they were first introduced into Britain is curious.

In the early 1950's an Italian dental mechanic, Pino Riservato, was in this country selling dental mirrors and other pieces of equipment. During his travels he became very familiar with what he called the 'snack-bar Inglese' and was appalled by the quality of the coffee they sold. He thought it was probably one of the chief reasons why the English were so fond of tea, and felt that there was great scope for espresso coffee.

Riservato was related by marriage to a director of the Gaggia Company in Milan, one of the many Italian firms manufacturing espresso machines, and was introduced through friends to an engineer who they thought would be the best person to help him look into the business prospects for selling Gaggia machines in this country. The firm of Riservato Partners Ltd. was formed, and five machines were ordered from Italy, destined, it so happened, for an eventful history.

When they arrived at Newhaven it was found that they should have had an import licence. No licence being forthcoming, the machines were shipped to Dublin. Riservato meanwhile came to an agreement with an alderman on the Isle of Man that the machines should be sent to the island and from there they found their way to the mainland. One of the five machines was set up in Riservato's flat in Jermyn Street in London, where it was demonstrated to caterers. All said they had seen or heard of this machine before in Italy, but they doubted if espresso coffee would be a good commercial proposition in Great Britain. They added that generally the British people were not interested in coffee, and even when they were, caterers were already fully capable of making it. Thus Riservato Partners Ltd. initially had no success in selling their machines, although from this problem another idea was born.

Instead of trying to fit the machines into the existing atmosphere of the snack bar with the stale tomato sandwiches and three-day-old Bath buns, it was decided to create a smart and clean coffee bar around the machines, and set an example which it was hoped would soon be copied. A Scotsman, Maurice Ross, was presented with the idea and he rented the bomb-damaged site of the Old Charlotte Laundry in Frith Street, Soho. With the help of an architect, Geoffrey Crockett, the first coffee bar was created.

The main feature of the interior, besides the espresso machine, was the cleanliness and contemporary decoration, which was all carried out in Formica, then an ultra-modern material. Only coffee, cakes and sandwiches were to be sold, and it was hoped that such an establishment would attract customers from the after-theatre and -cinema crowds. The future of the venture was uncertain, although there were 8,000 potential customers already in Soho, Italians who worked in hotels and restaurants in the area and who were used to espresso coffee at home.

The story of its opening became famous. People literally invaded the *Moka Bar* and over a thousand cups of coffee were served daily. Continental customers welcomed the opportunity to have black coffee, called *espresso*. The English, still wedded to their white coffee, drank *capuccino*, so called because it is the same colour as the habits worn by Capuchin friars. For *capuccino* coffee the milk was brought to boiling point by steam injection at approximately 20 lb. per square inch and creamed. This had obvious advantages over milk boiled in an urn, with its inevitable skin, and in addition had a certain attractiveness and novelty value. In fact, it was so attractive that it hoodwinked the English, and particularly the teenagers, into drinking something which was against all their traditional tea-drinking instincts. Three hundred thousand cups of coffee a year were sold in the *Moka Bar* during the first three years.

The first coffee bar outside Soho, and the second in London, was the *Coffee Inn*, opened by a man named Radmoski, a Polish Air Force pilot who lost an arm shortly after the Battle of Britain in a dog-fight over Le Havre. He had seen coffee houses in Warsaw after the war; his wife had also seen them in Switzerland. They thought the empty shop premises at 37 Park Lane would be ideal, and to overcome the import restriction an espresso machine was sent to them as a gift from relatives in Switzerland.

During a cocktail party given to celebrate its opening on Guy Fawkes night in 1952, passers-by, attracted by the lights and laughter and eager to see what was happening, formed a queue before the doors were actually opened. The three dozen continental pastries, which at the time were as rare as cream after the austere war years, were soon gone, and within the first few days they attracted 1,000 customers each day. Later Radmoski sold out and went to live in Canada.

The first coffee bar with contemporary décor was opened by Douglas Fisher, an interior decorator, and Cimatti, a wine merchant. They shared their idea, formed a partnership in June 1953 and after six months' preparation opened the *Mocamba* in Knightsbridge. It was a fabulous creation of bright décor, concealed lighting and lovely ceramics. A short spiral staircase joined the first and ground floors and very pretty and gaily dressed waitresses constantly walked up and down stairs serving cups of capuccino and espresso. Huge plates of continental gateaux were piled everywhere. Its opening

coincided with Coronation week and ensured its immediate popularity.

Other coffee bars of different shapes and sizes quickly followed.
There was *Il Capuccino* in George Street, the *Chalet* in Grosvenor
Street, the *Boulevard* in Wigmore Street and several in Soho. One of
the very early ones was the *Cabana* in Princess Street, and it set a
standard of décor, comfort and food for other coffee-bar restaurants,
that followed. It had clean-looking lines—rather like the restaurant

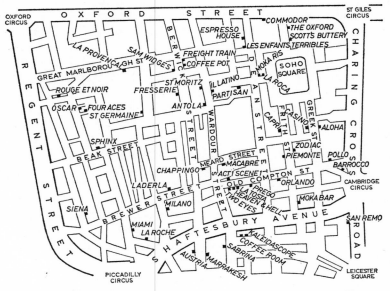

Map showing the locations of the coffee bars in Soho in the 'fifties.

of an ocean luxury liner—veneered, panelled walls from floor to
ceiling, soft lighting, Italian mirrors, soft-cushioned chairs, fans
and a false ceiling made of expanding metal over which were powerful extractors to overcome the usual restaurant smells. An additional
feature was a shop-window front which could be lifted and made to
disappear into the facia, leaving a continental style of frontage. A
pastry cook from Vienna was brought over specially to make pastries
on the premises. All went to create unprecedented comfort for an
eating place, and set a standard which guaranteed success to coffee-
bar restaurants of similar standing.

The spread of London coffee bars was very rapid. In the next
five years or so coffee bars became established as a feature of London
streets and in the provinces they proved just as popular. By 1960
there were over 2,000 of them, 500 in the Greater London area alone.

In the West End of London there were at least 200 coffee bars, and an employment bureau, opened specially to supply coffee bars with staff, did a roaring trade. London secretaries and even ex-débutantes found they could earn useful money by serving in coffee bars during the evening, and some of the smarter Knightsbridge coffee bars became famous for the beauty and aristocracy of their waitresses.

Many coffee bars were opened by firms specializing as tea and coffee suppliers and Kardomah and the Kenya Coffee Company have become well known. Kardomah, with dozens of coffee houses, are established all over the City, in Piccadilly and Knightsbridge as well as provincial cities. Kenya Coffee Company had establishments in the King's Road, Marylebone High Street, Sloane Street, Queensway and Knightsbridge.

The new coffee bars provided limitless scope for new styles of decoration, and ideas which had previously been seen only in nightclubs appeared above ground in Mayfair and Knightsbridge. The jungle had come to London, together with the Left Bank of the Seine, the Costa Brava and Montego Bay. There was a good deal of tiling, matting, wickerwork and wirework on view, and customers could even see rubber, cocoa and other tropical vegetation growing up the walls before their very eyes. Many coffee bars had a definite character, if not an actual national flavour, and the long-haired, corduroy-trousered community in Chelsea and Hampstead found a market for even its most modernistic flights of fancy.

There was keen competition among glass-makers and pottery-makers to torture their wares into ever newer and more fantastic shapes, and electricians performed wonders with lighting which ranged from the brilliant to the subterranean and unearthly. The hordes of enthusiastic young Londoners cheerfully dodged the hanging sculpture and filled alike the coffee bars whose main feature was comfort and those which seemed to concentrate on discomfort. They relived their continental holidays in settings which were more Italian than Italy and more Spanish than Spain.

The most exotic of the modern coffee bars was *El Cubano*, which lacked nothing. The proprietors, Cimmati and Fisher, had had to leave the *Mocamba*, which had been swallowed up in a road-widening scheme at Knightsbridge, and they reappeared 200 yards from Harrods in a Cuban coffee bar which attracted the attention of even the Cuban consul. Not only was there vegetation added to matting, stucco, marble and bamboo, there was an imitation of the parrot house at London Zoo and wild-life was provided to entertain the customers. The coffee was good. The menus were enormous and graded to suit every purse. There were Spanish guitars and air-conditioning and brightly dressed girls to serve the food. Downstairs there was a Roman room, and if there were not exactly orgies, there was certainly an orgy-like atmosphere. *El Cubano* was advertised as the most famous coffee house in Europe.

These were some of the more striking examples, and although they did good business at lunch-time, they were at their best during the evening. The personalities of the customers paled into insignificance against the eccentricities of the décor, but there were also other establishments which found themselves taking their characteristics from their clientele. They were usually patronised either by the artists and foreign students or the teenagers of the juke-box-playing persuasion.

The suburbs and provinces followed London's lead, but with slightly more moderation. There was already competition in most parts of the country from road-houses and old inns where 'character' had been a long-established feature, but, even so, the espresso machine fulfilled Riservato's confidence in its eventual success.

An interesting feature of the success story of the espresso machine is not only that the catering trade rejected the machine, describing it as that 'infernal machine', but that the idea and selling of the machine were being promoted by people like Riservato, who originally had no knowledge of the coffee trade. This aspect was, in fact, a feature of the whole coffee-bar growth. The foresight and the intuition came from people with little or no connection with catering, such as a wine merchant, an interior decorator, an antique dealer, a milliner, not to mention furriers, tailors, dentists, sculptors, psychiatrists and film stars. Perhaps it was a good thing that caterers had refused to use this machine, for had they done so it might well have been lost amid the conventional and uninteresting décor of an English café.

Why were the coffee bars so successful? For a wide selection of people they clearly fulfilled a need. They were excellent meeting places for young people. Office girls could chat happily with an escort; women shoppers and tourists found them handy and comfortable as resting places; business men could get a quick meal and they had no 'class' image.

Before the coffee bars opened there were few places in London which stayed open late enough for people to buy an after-theatre or -cinema snack in a pleasant atmosphere and at a reasonable price. The coffee bars filled the need, and it was said that they kept London awake at night. They were gay and offered continental or English food and a non-alcoholic drink, which many people preferred. Indeed, the coffee bars were badly needed.

Beans in their protective cover of parchment, being laid out to dry;
arabica coffee, East Africa.

Carrying the dried parchment back to the store.

Above, Picking out defective beans in the grading factory, Tanzania.

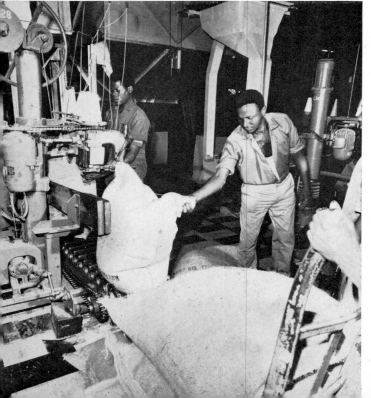

Left, Coffee which has had the parchment removed being automatically weighed and packed into bags.

Drawing samples for tasting, Tanzania.

Below, Coffee liquorers examining and tasting coffee before buying.

The interior of the Moka Bar in Soho, a type of coffee bar decor which became familiar to thousands of coffee drinkers during the coffee bar boom of the Fifties.

Two of the original coffee bars beneath the imposing mansions of Park Lane.

Many have travelled a long way from the transparent cups and Danish pastries, and it requires a good deal of courage to go into some of them and ask for just coffee between the hours of seven and ten in the evening. The decorations are expensive and it follows that the food is expensive too. The kitchens, and often the restaurants themselves, are equipped with every kind of modern spit roaster and the imposing menus are matched by equally imposing wine-lists. The wine licence has, in fact, lifted many of them almost out of the category of coffee bars altogether, although during the morning they can still be seen in their original guise, serving espresso and capuccino to elegant shoppers. The 'coffee restaurants' enjoy the best of all the catering worlds and even sell spit-roasted chickens to be taken home. They are to be found in every residential area where people habitually dine out and are willing to pay high prices for novelty and good food without the formality of the older, well-known restaurants.

In violent contrast were the juke-box coffee bars of Soho and the suburbs and provinces. Here the teenagers monopolized the place to the exclusion of every other type of customer. There was usually a distinct impression that the place had recently been beaten up. The lighting was much dimmer, the noise ten times louder and the clientele at least ten years younger. It was in one of these Soho coffee bars that Tommy Steele, among others, started his career. Teddy boys and teddy girls used to abound, but at first there was nothing about the coffee bars that was actually sinister, in spite of their rather forbidding aspect to people of an older generation.

The last distinct type of coffee bar was the one that had either a sideline or was incorporated into some other sort of business. There were coffee bars which sold delicatessen, tea and coffee, paintings and gramophone records. This indicated a trend on the part of the people who have to sell things—of an awareness of the value of having coffee available on the premises. The refreshment departments of many of the large stores installed espresso machines and hairdressers, cinema groups and public houses made use of them.

It would be tempting at this stage to say that the wheel of coffee history has come full circle, and the old coffee houses of the seventeenth and eighteenth centuries have resurrected themselves in the form of the modern coffee bar, but such an assumption would be misleading.

The coffee bars are not the cradles of business enterprises or the nurseries of new and progressive ideas, in spite of the bright young people who go to them. The coffee-bar clientele is usually about a generation younger than the men of Pepys's time, and women have

F

won their long-fought battle for the right to drink coffee with men. Certainly no Act of Parliament is ever likely to close them.

When coffee bars first appeared in London they received nothing but praise. They were bright, cheerful and popular. Then the extravagant décor showed signs of the passing of time. New ideas became rarer, and many of the new bars were content to be slightly jazzed-up versions of the familiar milk bar of ten years before. Perhaps this was inevitable. The espresso machine is no longer the attraction it was.

But young and old and foreigners too often complained about the coffee. They had doubts about the quality. The young people were not particularly impressed after the novelty had worn off; their elders never did like it. They protested about that bitter and often luke-warm frothy wash which was called espresso. Once or twice when I tried it the taste reminded me faintly of chewing the end of a pencil.

The proprietors of the coffee bars often blamed the coffee suppliers for not producing a more suitable blend. The coffee suppliers in turn blamed the proprietors for not buying the more expensive blends. The espresso sales agents said that the machine would maintain a high standard of coffee and that it could be counted on to produce the same brew at any time. Espresso machines are certainly capable of producing first-rate coffee if good-quality ground coffee is used and the machines are properly maintained, though as time went on they were joined by other methods of brewing coffee, which were more flexible in their treatment of different qualities and flavours. As coffee ceased to be the big novelty it had been in earlier years, the brewing machines occupied less-prominent positions in the coffee bars, which in fact made it easier for the staff to serve the customers and easier for the customers to see what was available for them to buy.

The excitement was over, but espresso machines had performed one big service for which they cannot be given too much credit. They introduced coffee to many of the British public and made them interested enough in it to want to make it themselves.

6

The Rise and Fall of the China Trade

The whole narrative is permeated with the odour of joss-sticks and honourable high-mindedness.

The Wallet of Kai Lung (Ernest Bramah)

One of the advertisements I answered on my return to London from Kenya was for a marketing man in a company dealing in Far Eastern trade. When I went along to be interviewed I found that there was a vacancy for someone to try to promote the sale of China tea to the United Kingdom. I knew something about Indian and Ceylon tea; African too, but China! That was something different.

My employers were a company recently formed to build up an import and export trade with the new People's Republic of China.

By 1949 the Chinese had stopped fighting their long series of civil wars; Chiang Kai-shek's Nationalist forces had withdrawn to Formosa and on the mainland the Communist regime of Mao Tse-tung reigned supreme. All the principal industries, including tea-growing, were promptly placed under state control. America remained a staunch supporter of the Nationalist Government in Formosa, and it became an offence for any American to trade with Red China. But after twenty years of war the new rulers of China faced a stupendous task in restoring the shattered economy, and they showed a fair degree of willingness to develop a two-way trade with Europe. They had to export in order to get foreign currency to pay for the foreign plant and equipment they badly needed.

In Britain, too, the new regime of Mao was viewed with considerable reserve, but both the established merchant houses in the Far Eastern Trade and newer companies took the view that political differences need not be a barrier to commerce.

One of the hopes of the Chinese lay in reviving the traditional

trade in China tea, a trade which had been steadily declining for
over half a century and which had ceased altogether during the
Second World War. I was twenty-five years old when it fell to me
to try to breathe life back into this extinct dinosaur and haul
the largest tea-producing country in the world and the greatest
tea-importing country in the world closer together.

To explain why it proved such a difficult task to restore the
flagging fortunes of China tea it is necessary to go back into history
and relate how, after enjoying a world monopoly for two whole
centuries and developing into a multi-million-pound business, it
fell on hard times.

The tea-growing areas of China.

The origin of the habit of tea-drinking goes back into Chinese
mythology. There are traditions attributing it to the Emperor
Shin Nong, who lived in the third millennium B.C., and a well-known
legend dating back to the fifth century A.D. about a Buddhist monk
named Dharuma who used to become sleepy when he was supposed
to be meditating. To punish himself, he cut off his eyelids, and
where they fell the first tea plants grew. Ever since, the Chinese
have believed that tea is a stimulant which will keep them
awake.

Certainly tea must have been well established long before the
eighth century, for in the year 780 the tea merchants of China

commissioned a prominent writer to produce a work extolling its merits. The result of this early essay in public relations was a book called *Ch'a Ching*, written by Lu-Yu, dealing exhaustively with every aspect of tea.

Europeans first heard about tea from various learned works of travel which were published during the sixteenth century, and one of the most important, translated into English from the Dutch, was a description by the navigator Jan Hugo van Linschooten of the custom of tea-drinking in China and Japan.

It was also the Dutch who first brought tea to Europe, and the first consignment is believed to have reached Holland in 1610. It was transported from Macao, the Portuguese foothold on the Chinese coast, to Java, and from there to Europe. The Dutch obtained it in a barter transaction, exchanging dry sage for tea. In 1618 the first tea reached Russia, to be followed later by the tea caravans travelling on the overland route across Central Asia. But for many years to come all the tea imported by sea was carried by the Dutch, and so it came about that when tea was at last introduced into England, a few years after coffee, all the early supplies were obtained from Holland.

Tea was first served to the public in England at Garraway's coffee house, by then a centre of mercantile transactions, in Change Alley in the City of London, in 1657. In the early days tea was brewed and kept in a cask, from which it was drawn and warmed up as the customers asked for it, but this method hardly did it justice.

With the Restoration of the Monarchy and the return of Charles II tea grew so rapidly in popularity that the Government of the day put a tax on it. It was an action which was to have far-reaching consequences more than a century later. About this time Samuel Pepys discovered tea. In 1660 he wrote in his diary: 'Did send for a cup of tea, a China drink which I had never drunk before.' Evidently he liked what he tasted, for by 1667 he was writing: 'Home, and there find my wife making of Tea.' Tea had quickly gained social status when it became known that Catherine of Braganza, consort of Charles II, drank it, having acquired the taste in her Portuguese homeland.

In 1664 the English East India Company presented Charles II with a gift of 2 lb. 2 oz. of tea, though even this was brought from Holland. Not until 1689 did the company realize that they were missing an important new market, when they started importing tea from China themselves. At first the company enjoyed a preference of 1s. 6d. (7p) per pound in duty, and in 1721 they were granted a monopoly of tea imports. These early teas were mostly high-quality green teas, although black teas from the Bohea Hills in China gained rapidly in favour and both sorts fetched up to 30s. (£1·50) per pound.

Meanwhile the Government thought they saw in tea a marvellous source of revenue. In the 100 years between 1711 and 1810 £77 million duty was collected on tea and duties ranged from 12½ to 200%. As a result, a flourishing smuggling industry grew up.

'Brandy for the parson, baccy for the clerk' is the popular conception of an eighteenth-century smuggler's stock-in-trade, but in fact tea was even more important. The decline of the coffee houses added to the popularity of tea, and by the middle of the century it had established its position as the national drink, the general non-alcoholic beverage of all classes of the community. By 1767 the tradition of early-morning tea was already quite common; one writer at the time stated that farmers' servants demanded tea for their breakfast. But it has been estimated that more than half the tea consumed in Britain at that time was contraband. The vast majority of people did not regard smuggling as a crime. Some of the East India Company's captains were involved in it, and even the revenue men could often be bribed to keep out of the way when contraband tea was on the move.

The coasts of Hampshire and Dorset, with their many isolated coves and inlets, were one of the main centres of this illicit but highly organized trade. In those relatively few instances where the revenue men were both efficient and incorruptible the smugglers received no quarter if they were unlucky enough to get caught.

In the churchyard of St. Andrew's Church at Kinson, just north of what is now Bournemouth, there is a tombstone with the following inscription:

To the memory of
Robert Trotman

Late of Rond in the county of Wilts who was
barbarously murdered on the shore near Poole
on the 24 March, 1765

A little tea one leaf I did not steal
For guiltless blood shed I to God appeal
Put tea in one scale, human blood in t'other
And think what 'tis to slay thy harmless brother.

Even smuggled tea was expensive. In 1777 it was fetching

10s. 6d. (53p) per pound and this inevitably led to another abuse, that of adulteration. Green teas were adulterated with processed leaves of willow, sloe and elder, and also with 'smouch'—an obnoxious preparation made from ash leaves. Tea leaves which had already been used once and dried were also added to the new tea. It was a profitable business, in spite of heavy fines imposed by special laws, for by this time annual tea consumption had risen to 2 lb. per head.

The situation was so ludicrous that in 1784 William Pitt, who had become Prime Minister in the previous year, resorted to bold action. He slashed the import duty on tea to $12\frac{1}{2}\%$, and smuggling disappeared, but not in time to save the American colonies.

Tea was introduced into New England almost as soon as into the mother country. In New York it was being drunk by the Dutch while the settlement was still called Nieuw Amsterdam, before it was annexed by the British in 1664. From 1765 onwards the British Government made desultory efforts to raise taxation from the American colonists, largely to pay for the recent wars against the French and the Indians, from which the colonists, of course, had benefited. In 1767 it was proposed to levy duties on American imports of four commodities, paper, glass, lead and tea. This raised a storm of protest from the colonial assemblies, and the Government agreed to abandon the duties with the fateful exception of tea, which was to be taxed at 3d. (1p) per pound.

Instead of paying it, the colonists simply smuggled tea across the Atlantic from Holland. Faced with the competition of American smugglers as well as English, the East India Company found itself with large stocks of surplus tea, so from the Parliament at Westminster they secured an Act allowing them to ship tea to America direct, without payment of English duty.

Boston had from the start been a centre of American resistance to British rule and it was here, as luck would have it, that the first three cargoes to be shipped direct from China arrived in December 1773. The East India Company's agents were waiting to receive the tea, but the colonists would not allow it to be unloaded. The unfortunate ship's captains, however, were under orders not to sail until the cargoes had been discharged.

Tempers flared, and then under cover of darkness, on the night of the 16th December, a group of Americans disguised as Red Indians boarded the vessels, seized the 342 chests of tea and threw all £10,000 worth into the waters of Boston harbour. This was the Boston Tea Party which sparked off the American War of Independence. Events moved rapidly after that. The Americans organized a boycott of all British goods, the British retaliated by attempting to enforce martial law. The colonists laid in supplies of arms against the day of revolution. In 1775 the war started and in 1776 the first Continental Congress drew up the Declaration of Independence.

From having been the favourite American drink, tea became the hated symbol of oppression. To refuse to drink tea was the mark of the American patriot, and ever since the night of the Boston Tea Party the Americans have always drunk more coffee than tea. Yet in Canada, which remained loyal to the British Crown, tea continued to be a popular drink.

Back in England, the low rate of duty on tea did not last long. In 1795 it was back to 25% and there followed successive steep rises until by 1806 it was no less than 96%, almost as much as before Pitt's reform. But, or course, these were the times of the French wars and the menace of Napoleon. The need to raise revenue was urgent.

Tea was still sold to the public loose from the chests, but eventually the mixing or blending of teas from different chests became popular to stabilize quality. This was done by the grocer before he offered the tea for sale. Many famous businesses started in a modest way as tea blenders, among them Harrods, Fortnum and Mason and Jackson's of Piccadilly. Cadbury's originally sold tea, and the Isle of Wight firm of Upward and Rich, established in 1650, who claim to be one of the three oldest grocery firms in the country.

A return to high taxation meant also a return by unscrupulous traders to the malpractice of adulteration. Before long, pure tea became almost unobtainable, and the whole tea trade acquired an unenviable reputation for sharp practice.

To remedy this state of affairs, John Horniman, an Isle of Wight trader, became in 1826 the first man to sell tea in sealed quarter-pound and half-pound packets which he guaranteed to contain only pure and unadulterated tea. The packets were of paper, lead-lined. At first they were filled by hand, but later he invented a crude packing machine which he used until the growth of the business necessitated its removal to London. Although the enterprise of John Horniman and other traders who followed his example helped to eliminate adulteration by people in this country, there was a thriving adulteration industry in China which was more difficult to stop.

The Chinese, too, used to save the leaves from their teapots, dry them and add them to the chests of new tea to increase the weight. This exhausted tea was called 'maloo' and the real tea was further diluted by 'li', which was a substance which looked like tea but was really made from some other plant.

Eventually, the Food and Drugs Act of 1875 made the importing of adulterated tea an offence, and to enforce the new regulations the Government appointed an examiner who inspected tea entering the Customs House. As soon as it was realized that tea not passed by the examiner was liable to seizure and destruction, the situation rapidly improved.

The third and fourth decades of the nineteenth century were crucial years when the modern tea industry as we know it today began to cast its shadows before it, for just seven years after John Horniman put his bright idea into practice the East India Company's monopoly of the China trade was brought to an end.

This trade had flourished largely because the East India Company known as 'John Company' had organized the cultivation of opium and forced it on the Chinese to make them export their tea and silk in exchange. Both importers in London and merchants who wanted a share of the China trade, including the opium trade, bitterly resented the monopoly of the East India Company and its arrogance, particularly as its tottering finances were continually having to be shored up by the British Government at the taxpayer's expense. By the 1830's the clamour for the monopoly to be abolished was impossible to resist and the Government yielded.

In this new situation the East India Company looked around for an alternative source of tea supplies, preferably one under their own control, and they found one almost straight away on their own territory in India. Their monopoly there had ended in 1813, earlier than in China, but they still maintained the largest private army in history and exercised the curious but convenient dual function of merchants and administrators.

Back in 1788 the botanist Sir Joseph Banks had recommended the cultivation of tea in Assam in northern India, but while the company retained its profitable monopoly of the China trade the idea was forgotten. It was, after all, much easier to let the Chinese do all the work. In 1822 the Royal Society of Arts offered fifty guineas (£52·50) to whoever could grow and prepare the greatest quantity of China tea in the British West Indies, Cape of Good Hope, New South Wales or the East Indies. The prize remained unclaimed, yet all the time indigenous tea plants were growing wild in Assam, and in 1823 they were discovered by Major Robert Bruce in the course of a trading expedition to that part of India. For many years the Singhpos, one of the hill tribes on the Burma border, had used Assam tea, made in the Burmese way, by pickling it.

The British had not really wanted to govern Assam, which was to them a commercially useless area tucked away in the north-east corner of India and in a state of perpetual war between rival rajahs, but when a group of Ahom rajahs called in the Burmese to help them, the British were obliged to intervene. The Assamese had a reputation for ruthlessness, but their cruelties were nothing compared with the atrocities committed by the Burmese. In 1824 the British wrested Assam from the Burmese in the First Burma War and since none of the Assam rajahs could be trusted to rule competently if unsupervised, they completed the operation by establishing garrisons supported by gunboats in the Brahmaputra Valley.

When the East India Company's monopoly was abolished in 1833 it was replaced by a Charter Act which contained two important provisions allowing British subjects freedom to trade and also to settle in India, which they had previously been forbidden to do. Before this date there could have been no cultivation of tea by the British, and even Robert Bruce's explorations were only possible because he was an employee of the East India Company and a major in the Bengal Artillery. In 1834 Lord William Bentinck, the Governor of Bengal and also Governor-General of India, appointed a Tea Committee to submit 'a plan for the accomplishment of the introduction of tea cultivation into India, and for the superintendence of its execution'. Robert Bruce, meanwhile, had died, but he had passed on his knowledge of native Assam tea to his brother, C. A. Bruce, who did all the pioneering work of finding out how to grow and make tea.

The Tea Committee reported that they were sure that tea in India would be a commercial proposition, but their conclusions about suitable areas for cultivation were often mistaken and the mysteries of tea manufacture were hardly understood at all. C. A. Bruce was made Superintendent of Tea Culture, a Government appointment, and although he was by now an expert on Assam tea, it was decided that China plants were to be imported from China.

In 1839 their efforts were rewarded when the first eight chests of Indian tea were sold at the London auctions. Small as the amount may have been, it was this epoch-making event which set in train the decline of the China tea trade. The *Asiatic Journal* described the events of January 10th:

'The first importation of tea from the British territories in Assam, consisting of eight chests containing about 350 lb., was put up by the East India Company to public sale in the commercial salerooms, Mincing Lane, and excited much curiosity. The lots were eight, three of Assam souchong and five of Assam pekoe. On offering the first lot (souchong) Mr. Thompson, the sale broker, announced that each lot would be sold without the least reservation to the highest bidder. The first bid was 5s. [25p] per pound, a second bid was made of 10s. [50p] per pound. After much competition it was knocked down for 21s. [£1·05] per pound the purchaser being Captain Pidding. The second lot of souchong was bought for the same person for 20s. (£1, or 100p) per pound. The third and last lot of souchong sold for 16s. [80p] per pound, Captain Pidding being the buyer. The first lot of Assam pekoe sold after much competition for 24s. [£1·20] per pound, every broker appearing to bid for it; it was bought for Captain Pidding. The second, third and fourth lots of Assam pekoe fetched the respective prices of 25s. [£1·25], 27s. 6d. [£1·37] and 28s. 6d. [£1·43] per pound and were also purchased for Captain Pidding. For the last lot (pekoe) a most exciting competition took place—there were nearly sixty bids made for it. It was at last knocked down at the extraordinary price of 34s. [£1·70] per pound. Captain Pidding was also the purchaser of this lot, and has therefore become the sole proprietor of the first importation of Assam tea. This gentleman, we understand, has been induced to give this enormous price for an article that may be produced at 1s. [5p] per pound by the public-spirited motive of securing a fair trial to this valuable product of British Assam.'

Captain Pidding was the proprietor of the 'Howqua Mixture' named after a Chinese tea merchant in Canton who was reputed to be worth more than £5 million. The eight chests which he bought were divided into small samples and distributed at 2s. 6d. (13p) each to advertise the new tea.

A second lot of ninety-five chests arrived late in 1839 and showed much improved quality. Several buyers showed a keen interest, among them Messrs. Twining and Co., and the price was pushed up to between 8s. (40p) and 11s. (55p) per pound. Twinings thought the tea had a strong and useful flavour and said that they were certain that more experience in the culture and manufacture would result in a tea fully equal to the finer descriptions of China tea. This was the general opinion of all the importers and foreshadowed the beginning of the end of China tea in this country.

It is significant, although at the time no one realized this, that the tea sent in these first two shipments was made from the native Assam plant, as the newly planted China tea was not ready for plucking.

The new tea from India was helped by the changeover in public taste from green tea to black as people became aware of the adulteration of their tea. From the beginning, most of the tea manufactured in India was black tea and had the advantage of at least looking familiar.

The Indian Government's experimental tea gardens were handed over to the Assam Company in 1840, and to make sure that they had the most favourable start the corrupt native ruler was deposed and the province of Assam annexed on behalf of the British Crown. But there were still many problems to be overcome. The art of growing tea belonged exclusively to the Chinese and the Assam Company had to learn it the hard way. The region was extremely unhealthy, and the mortality among Europeans and native labourers from cholera and plague was appalling. Transport difficulties were immense and the cost of clearing the jungle for tea plantations proved far higher than expected. By 1847 the Assam Company was on the verge of bankruptcy, but more money was raised and in the following year the prospect was brighter. In 1852 the Company declared its first dividend. It was only a humble 2½% but it proved that Indian tea was here to stay. So was the Assam Company, although its famous parent, the East India Company, was taken over by the British Government in 1858 as one of the results of the Indian Mutiny.

The Mutiny came as a nasty shock to the British, who had assumed that the Indians did not mind being colonised by a foreign power and exploited by the East India Company's nabobs, but it did not extend to Assam, which during the 1850's had enough troubles of its own.

The Assam Company's manager, George Williamson, wrote to his directors in Calcutta:

'. . . The difficulties are at present enhanced by the descent of the Bhutias into Durrang on the one hand, and the apprehension of invasion by the Burmese on the other hand, which with the ravages of cholera on all sides has created a sort of panic throughout the Province.'

George Williamson is one of the great figures in the history of tea. When he first took over management of the Assam Tea Company estates in 1847 things were in a bad way, but in a few years he had pulled them round. Williamson was certain that the root of the trouble was the 'cursed China jat' and he decided to replace it with selected Assam jat. 'Jat' is a hindustani word meaning 'caste'. His directors were alarmed at first, but Williamson was proved right and in 1856 the company was able to pay a dividend of 9%. This momentous step was the first of several which were to free Indian tea production from centuries-old misconceptions about tea cultivation imposed by Chinese tradition. The British developed their own theories based on sound horticulture and Indian tea became a tea in its own right, and not inferior China tea.

The eventual success of the Assam Company and of the Jorehaut Tea Company which followed it in 1858 encouraged the opening up of tea estates by both private individuals and companies with famous names whose share prices are still quoted daily in the plantation section of the financial columns.

Even so, the greatest, most dramatic, days of China tea were still to come. Although China's share of the total market gradually fell in percentage terms, her tea production for export continued to increase, reaching its peak in the 1880's.

When the East India Company started its tea trade with China in the early years of the eighteenth century the Chinese Emperor only allowed trade with foreigners through the port of Canton. The Chinese side of all trading transactions was carried on by a group of Chinese merchants, always thirteen in number, who were known as the 'hong merchants' because of their hongs, or warehouses, near to the factories of the foreign merchants.

There were thirteen of these factories ranged along the water-front, one for the British, one for the French, one for the Dutch and so on, each flying its national flag and each with its dock from which sampans could take the packed tea and bales of silks down the Pearl River to the Whampoa Anchorage, ten miles away, beyond which no foreign ship was allowed to approach the city. At this time the tea for export arrived in Canton from the farmers in a partly manufactured state. The hong merchants then had it finished ready to be bought by the foreign agents. Common black tea was called 'hong-cha'.

Several European countries had their own East India Companies which allowed lesser merchants to trade under licence, and between them these merchants supplied the tea for the whole world outside the Far East. The Chinese hong merchants amassed huge fortunes in the 130 years of their ascendancy, in particular Howqua, who was born in poverty in Amoy in 1769, joined the co-hong while he was still in his twenties, and by 1825 was recognized as the doyen of the thirteen hong merchants. His home was one of the show-places of old Canton, and he earned for himself the title of the Chinese Croesus. When one of his supervisors embezzled over £10,000 from an American merchant, Howqua made immediate restitution. The foreigners were much impressed, but Howqua could afford the occasional honest gesture, for although the co-hong had the reputation of being scrupulous in their financial dealings in the days when written agreements were unknown, their honesty and fair dealing had well-defined limits.

Sir John Francis Davis in his book *The Chinese*, published in 1840, says: 'The remission of the tea duties in the United States occasioned, in the years 1832 and 1833, a demand for green teas at Canton, which would not be supplied by the arrivals from the provinces. The Americans, however, were obliged to sail with cargoes of green teas within the favourable season; they were determined to have these teas; and the Chinese were determined they should be supplied. Certain rumours being afloat concerning the manufacture of green tea from old black leaves the writer of this became curious to ascertain the truth, and with some difficulty persuaded a hong merchant to conduct him, accompanied by one of his inspectors, to the place where the operation was carried on.' What Sir John found was that large quantities of black tea which had been damaged in floods the previous autumn were being dried and refired and treated with turmeric, sulphate of lime and prussian blue to make a very convincing imitation of a high-quality green tea. The first two chemicals were believed, in 1840 at least, to be harmless, but the prussian blue, being a combination of prussic acid and iron, is a poison. In addition to this type of fraud, there is no doubt that the hong merchants swelled their enormous fortunes by exploiting their lesser countrymen. In turn, the Chinese Government extorted large amounts of money from the co-hong.

The co-hong system was finally abolished by the Treaty of Nanking after the Opium War of 1842, when trade was opened up in other ports and many British firms joined in the expansion of the China trade. Before that date the only part of China where foreigners could set foot was the small strip of waterfront in Canton harbour occupied by their own factories which also consisted of offices and living quarters. For the next half-century the China tea industry was prosperous and the British merchants could pick the best from the hundreds of high-quality teas which were available. Closer supervision improved the reliability of these export teas, but in spite of the efforts of explorers and horticulturalists like Robert Fortune, the Chinese were reluctant to divulge all the secrets of their tea-manufacturing methods and some of these always remained a mystery.

The period 1860 to 1880 was the hey-day of the caravan trade between China and Russia. Some camel trains started from Peking, but mostly the tea was sent from Hankow to Tientsin by sea and then either loaded on to camels in Tientsin or sent by junk up the Pei-ho River to Tungchow to join the camel train there. Caravans of

200 to 300 beasts would then cross the 800 miles of the Gobi Desert to Kiakhta on the North Chinese border and enter Russia via Irkutsk, then on to Nij-Udinsk, Tomsk and Oomsk to Cheliabinsk. The entire 11,000-mile journey took sixteen months, but in some curious way the caravan teas which reached Britain acquired enormous prestige. Apparently it was believed that several weeks of sea voyage deteriorated the tea more than several months of contact with hot camel. This legend, like other China tea legends, died hard. The last camel caravan left Peking in 1900, when the final link in the Trans-Siberian Railway was completed, but, in spite of this, genteel characters in books continued to drink caravan tea for many years afterwards.

As time went on, Shanghai became the chief port for the export of tea, as it was more convenient than Canton for collecting and loading the marks of China black congou tea which the British firms found most suitable for British tastes. For a long time Shanghai was chief of the treaty ports and the main centre of British influence in China next to the colony of Hong Kong.

The special importance of the China tea trade created a special class of merchant ship to serve its needs. With the abolition of the East India Company's monopoly, British shippers began to look for faster vessels than the huge, splendidly equipped, but slow and cumbersome East Indiamen. In 1849 the British Navigation Laws were repealed, allowing American vessels to trade into British ports for the first time.

The Americans for some years past had been developing a new kind of sailing ship, a three-masted, full-rigged vessel with fine lines and a great turn of speed. Their original inspiration came from the privateers of the short-lived Anglo-American War of 1812, and so the famous clippers were born.

The *Oriental* was the first American clipper to ply between China and England, and the London tea merchants were amazed when she arrived in London in the autumn of 1850 with her 1,600 tons of tea, only ninety-seven days out from Hong Kong. She was soon joined by other California clippers. British shipowners realized that if they were not to be ousted from their own trade they would have to build clipper ships on American lines. The first British clipper was *Stornoway*, built in Aberdeen in 1850. She was commissioned by Jardine, Matheson & Co. still to this day a famous merchant house in the Far Eastern trade. The *Stornoway* was followed by several fast British clippers, but throughout the 1850's the Americans held the ascendancy with a superb series of California clippers designed by Donald McKay of Boston. Because of their enormous spread of

sail they could achieve astonishing speeds. *Lightning*, one of a quartet
of McKay ships commissioned for the Australia packet lines, made
436 nautical miles in twenty-four hours, a record for a sailing ship
which has never been beaten. She was a 'Blackballer', a ship of the
Black Ball line which was notorious for the harshness of its captains.

Then in the 1860's, with America occupied with a civil war,
British shipbuilders took over the lead and American competition
was diverted to the more profitable transatlantic passenger business,
carrying gold prospectors to California and Irish emigrants to
Philadelphia. Starting with *Falcon* in 1859, twenty-six tea fliers were
built in British shipyards during the next ten years, notably by
Robert Steele & Co. of Greenock and Alexander Hall & Co. of
Aberdeen. The most successful clippers established an imperishable
place in Britain's maritime history and their pictures by J. Spurling
and other painters, skysails and stunsails set and breasting tumul-
tuous waves, have adorned walls and calendars for a century.

1866 was the year of the most celebrated tea race of all. Throughout the sixties several ships had won reputations for fast speeds
and at the beginning of May they were all waiting to be loaded
in the Min River. Tea was also shipped from Hong Kong, Amoy,
Shanghai and Canton at this time, but the main competition
was between the dozen first-class tea clippers gathered at the
Pagoda Anchorage below Foochow. While the English agents and
Chinese merchants haggled over the price of the tea in Foochow, all
ropes and sails were checked, the ballast was levelled and covered
by a layer of chests of inferior tea to protect the choice 'chops' when
they arrived. The house flag of the owners flew from the main
masts, the captains' pennants from the mizzens, and from practically
every ship the British Ensign on a flagstaff over the taffrail. As soon
as the first contracts were made, the chests were packed, labelled and
rushed off on sampans twelve miles downriver to the clippers, and
a handful chosen as the 'going ships' were loaded first.

The prize for the captain and crew of the winning ship was £500,
for the owners of the first new season's consignment to reach London
reaped handsome profits, and the tea would fetch as much as 6d.
(3p) per pound more than tea from slower ships. By 9 a.m. on the
day after the first ship arrived samples would be available for
bids in Mincing Lane and that night the first chests would be
on their way by rail to be on sale in all the big cities of Britain
next morning. Many ships were lost after only a few voyages, but
so valuable was their cargo that they paid for themselves after two
or three years and the captains took great risks to clip a few days off
the run. The clippers were tricky to handle, being very narrow for

A coffee bar in the evening. For the first time young people had a place they could go to which was cheap and warm and catered specially for their needs.

The sort of decor which reminded customers of continental holidays and distinguished the new coffee bar from the old milk bars.

The Canton factories of the foreign merchants ranged along the water-front. Each factory had living quarters and luxurious rooms for entertaining.

The earliest method of firing tea in China. For centuries tea production changed very little.

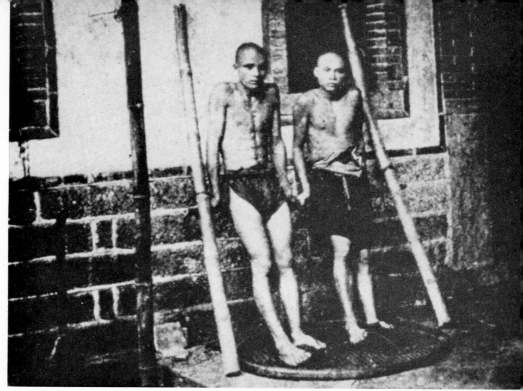

Above, Early photograph showing Chinese coolies rolling tea with their feet. The tea produced by such primitive methods was often of a very high quality and had an infinite variety of flavours.

Right, A camel caravan leaving Peking for its 800 mile journey across the Gobi Desert to Russia. The last caravan left in 1900 when the Trans Siberian Railway was completed.

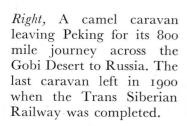

Sequence of drawings showing tea production in Ceylon. Reproduced from the *Graphic* magazine, January 1888.

their length, and many were too fine astern to make them safe in a following sea. In heavy weather the crew were always in danger of being washed overboard.

In 1866 there were three ships which had 'form' and the race was expected to between them. *Fiery Cross* had won in 1861, 1862 and 1863, and her master, Captain Robinson, had the most formidable reputation in the China Seas. *Serica* won from *Fiery Cross* in 1864 and would have won in 1865 too had not Captain Robinson had the luck to secure a tug off Beachy Head when he was two miles astern and been towed to London Docks ahead of his rival. The fastest passage that year was by *Taeping*, which had made too late a start to take part in the race but was a ship to reckon with. Lastly there was a new ship, *Ariel*. Captain Keay, her master, had had great success with *Falcon* and *Ellen Rodgers* and there were rumours later that he had doubled his crew. In fact this was not so; he carried a picked crew of thirty-two able seamen, only two more than usual, and his first officer, Duncan, was considered the smartest racing mate in the whole fleet. *Ariel*, *Serica* and *Taeping* were all Robert Steele ships and by 1866 the annual event had become a one-class yacht race.

On the 28th May 1866 *Ariel*, first to finish loading, led her rivals out of the Pagoda Anchorage, but *Fiery Cross* passed her and was soon out to sea with a day's start. *Serica* and *Taeping* joined *Ariel* and they crossed the bar of the Min River together. The strong winds in the China Seas and Indian Ocean separated the ships, but although at Mauritius *Fiery Cross* was still a day ahead, all were making fast daily runs, often over 300 miles a day. After rounding the Cape, the four ships drew closer together and at St. Helena *Taeping* had taken the lead. Then on 9th August they ran into doldrum weather and *Taeping* and *Fiery Cross* were becalmed within sight of each other with *Ariel* to the west. For eight days they languished until a breeze from the west picked them up, *Ariel* first, and drove them to the Azores, only a day separating them at Flores.

Captain Keay in *Ariel* was barely maintaining his lead as he proceeded with all possible sail and he had no illusions about the quality of his opposition. In the early hours of 5th September he logs the Bishop and St. Agnes lights and makes this ominous entry: 'A ship, since daylight, has been in company on starboard quarter—*Taeping* probably.' All day the two ships raced up the Channel, according to Captain Keay 'Going 14 knots royal stunsails and flying kites set and wind strong from W.S.W.' *Serica* meanwhile was coming up on the French side. From each headland news of their positions was telegraphed to the owners and agents

G

waiting in London to rush down to the appropriate dock to greet the winning ship.

As she neared Dungeness early on the morning of the 6th September *Ariel* began to burn blue lights and send up rockets for a pilot. Two cutters came out from Dungeness to meet the clippers, and *Ariel*, seeing *Taeping* also signalling, tacked in between her and the cutters and took her pilot first. Captain Keay was therefore the winner of the race under sail, but the race was not over. The prize went to the first ship to heave its sample chest over the side at the London Docks and the importance of this last stage was not lost on Captain Keay, who wrote in his log: '5.55. Rounded to close to the pilot cutter and got first pilot. Were saluted as first ship from China this season. I replied, "Yes, and what is that to the westward? We have not room to boast yet. Thank God we are first up Channel and hove to for a pilot an hour before him." '

By this time the owners of the leading ships were in such a state of agitation in London that they decided that whatever the outcome of the race the prize should be shared. However, Captain Keay and Captain McKinnon of *Taeping* knew nothing of this and as they raced on excitement on the two ships was intense. At six o'clock Captain Keay writes: 'Hoisted our number abreast of Deal we were then fully a mile ahead of *Taeping* and kept so until obliged to take in all sail to take steamer ahead.' From this point *Taeping* took the lead. She may have had the faster tug, but more probably *Ariel*'s greater weight made all the difference. She was 150 tons heavier and carried the most tea of all the leading ships. Also she was lower in the water, and this was crucial. There was a rising tide and, however fast her tug, she would have to wait until there was enough water for her to dock. It was a harrowing finish for Captain Keay, although his log betrays no hint of his disappointment.

'*Taeping* reached Gravesend fifty-five minutes before us. We avoided anchoring by getting a tug alongside to keep us astern. Proceeded with first tug ahead, as the flowing tide gave us sufficient water to float, thus reached Blackwall and East India Dock entrance at 9 p.m. Could not open the gates till tide rose higher. 10.23 p.m. Hove the ship inside dock gates. *Taeping* had preceded us up the river, but, having farther to go, did not reach the entrance of London Docks till 10 p.m. and, drawing less water than we, also dock having two gates, they got her inside outer gate, shut it, and allowed the lock to fill from the dock, then opened the inner gate so she docked some twenty minutes before us—the papers have it half an hour, for the sake of precision.'

Serica reached the West India Dock at eleven-thirty, just as the gates were being closed, making a neat conclusion to the Great Tea Race. The three ships which had crossed the bar of the Min River on the same tide had all docked in London ninety-nine days later on the same tide.

The race of 1866, though the greatest, was also one of the last. Three years later the Suez Canal was opened, making large steamers in Eastern seas an economic proposition for the first time. The early steamships were gluttons for coal and such was the expense of maintaining coaling stations that they had hitherto mainly concentrated on passengers and mails. The Canal made all the difference, and Alfred Holt's Blue Funnel steamers quickly captured the cream of the tea trade.

In 1867 *Ariel* was the undisputed winner from Foochow, although *Sir Lancelot* arrived in London first after a ninety-nine day voyage from Shanghai. *Spindrift* won from *Ariel* in 1868 and in 1869 *Sir Lancelot* was first from Foochow in a record eighty-nine days. The final tea race took place in 1871 and the remaining clippers were either sold to other countries or transferred to the Australia run, carrying passengers outwards and wool homewards. The four leaders of 1866 all came to an untimely end. *Fiery Cross* caught fire at Sheerness, *Serica* was wrecked in 1869 and *Taeping* foundered on Ladds Reef on her way from Amoy to New York. *Ariel*, the most famous clipper of her day, was described by Basil Lubbock, the authority on sailing ships, as always ticklish to handle. 'If overpressed she had a habit of settling down aft and had to be quickly relieved of her mizzen canvas or she would drown her helmsman. This fault was due to a want of bearing aft, which was practically the only flaw in Robert Steele's tea-ship designs.' It was a defect which proved disastrous. In 1872 she left London for Sydney laden with emigrants and was never heard of again. She was always at her most difficult in the 'Roaring Forties' and it was supposed that 'she broached to and foundered when running her easting down'. *Spindrift* was wrecked in 1869 and *Sir Lancelot* foundered in a cyclone in the Bay of Bengal in 1895.

Some of the clippers went under the Portuguese flag, and today the only survivor of these is the *Cutty Sark*, built to compete with a lovely ship called *Thermopylae*, but launched too late to take part in the heyday of the China trade. She returned to England in 1922 to become a training ship at Falmouth, and now she is ending her days as a tourist attraction in dry dock at Greenwich.

*   *   *   *   *

Throughout the 1860's the Indian tea plantations expanded rapidly,

extending from Assam into several other parts of India, notably
Darjeeling, Cachar and Sylhet, thus originating some of the world's
most famous teas which are still highly prized. By 1875 about
125,000 acres were under tea cultivation in India, and annual
production had risen to £26 million.

It was about this time that mechanization was successfully
introduced into Assam to solve the perpetual labour shortage. In
the early days an attempt had been made to import several hundred
Chinese from the bazaars and waterfronts of Calcutta and Singapore.
They had no experience of tea-making and must have been employed
on the principle that any Chinaman was better than none. There are
many men in tropical agriculture who have been driven to drink by
a Chinese labour force, but these were bad by any standards.
Fifty-seven landed in jail and the rest went back to Calcutta, where
they were rounded up by the police and deported. They were replaced by Indians, who were more reliable but totally inexperienced.
Since tea was still being manufactured by the Chinese method, by
far the largest proportion of labour was engaged in rolling leaf,
either with their feet or between the palms of their hands.

Several British plantation managers tried to invent machines
which would do the job more efficiently and hygienically, and the
most successful was William Jackson, a young Scotsman who set
up his first tea roller in 1872 on the Heeleakah Garden of the Scottish
Assam Tea Company. He followed it with a series of improved rollers
and other machinery which reduced the cost of tea production from
11d. (5p) per pound in 1872 to 2½d. (1p) or 3d. (1p) per pound in
1913. By this time 8,000 rolling machines were able to do the work
which would previously have required a million and a half coolies,
and without them any large-scale expansion of the estates would
have been impossible.

At the same time that Jackson was introducing his rollers,
Samuel Davidson, in another part of Assam, was experimenting with
tea driers and this led him on to mechanize all the stages of tea
manufacture. Both young men formed companies to produce their
machines and between them they revolutionized Indian tea manufacture to the same extent that Williamson had transformed tea
cultivation twenty years before and carried it forward into the
twentieth century.

As the estates built tea factories on modern lines, more and more
labour was freed to concentrate on proper terracing, weeding and
pruning, which rapidly improved the quality of the plant. The
flavour of Indian tea was rather stronger than the China tea to
which the British public was accustomed, and in the early days it

was mixed with China tea, adding new importance to the tea blender's trade.

In the 1870's another new producer, Ceylon, arose to challenge further the domination of China tea. Ceylon's prosperity had been based on coffee, but in 1869 the dreaded coffee blight began to attack the plants and within ten years the entire industry had been devastated. One of the coffee planters, James Taylor, another Scotsman who was an assistant on the Loolecondera Estate, planted a few acres of tea from Assam seed. His first experiments with tea started in 1867 and he found out how to pluck, wither and roll the tea from planters who had lived in India, providing a lead which was followed by other planters when their coffee crops were hit. The climatic and soil conditions proved to be ideal for tea-growing and with great courage and determination the planters set about making a success of their new crop. Since then the high-grown teas from the mountain slopes of Ceylon have achieved a world reputation for their superior quality. By 1895 the island's tea estates covered 300,000 acres.

During a similar period Dutch planters in Java, encouraged by their Government, had been experimenting with tea. As early as the 1830's they had tried the China jat, or variety of tea plant, then they planted seed from Japan, but neither of these strains proved entirely successful. The new British plantations in Assam provided the answer. The sturdier Assam jat, took the place of the China plants and improvements in the manufacture of the tea solved the remaining problems.

Even in the early part of the nineties Britain still obtained about a third of her tea from China, but inexorably the Empire teas gained ground. To the London merchants they had a special attraction, as import duty applied only to foreign teas, and Indian and Ceylon teas, being Empire produce, came in duty free. They also preferred the way in which Empire teas were sent to London as soon as they were ready and put up for auction under the name of the producing company and the estate. China teas were sold by the small farmers to local collectors and then to Chinese merchants and might pass through several hands before a British importer brought them to London, by which time their history was sometimes rather obscured, although the agents of the British merchants had their own system of grading tea. Some oriental merchants bought and sold China teas among themselves rather in the same manner that Mark Twain's people made a precarious living by taking in one another's washing.

Up to 1890 the agents of British importers held a commanding

position in the great China tea market of Hankow, the inland tea
port 600 miles up the Yangtze west of Shanghai. But after that
date British purchasers declined drastically. In 1892 only four
British vessels called at Hankow to load cargoes of North China
congous, and in 1901 there was none at all. The competition
of duty-free tea from India and Ceylon was having its inevitable
effect.

The trend was hastened by developments on the home market.
In Mincing Lane wholesalers became established, doing their own
blending, and the first proprietary blends of tea appeared, introducing brand names that became household words. For this type
of trade the blenders preferred tea from India and Ceylon, reliable
and consistent in quality and cheaper in price. After 1900 the
grocery chains were gradually developed, selling tea only in blended
packet form.

As early as 1884 Mazawattee launched their packet of pure
Ceylon tea, promoted by heavy advertising. Advertising was to be
one of this company's strengths, and in 1891 they bought a consignment of Gartmore 'golden tips' tea at the Mincing Lane auctions
at the then world record price of £25 10s. (£25·50) per pound to
demonstrate to the public the quality of the tea they were prepared
to buy. Mazawattee's buyer on this occasion was known ever afterwards in the trade as 'Golden Tips Jackson' and there is a tradition
in the firm that some of this tea was presented by Queen Victoria to
Princess Mary and the Duke of York on the occasion of their
marriage in 1893. A large advertisement was published, showing
the Queen presenting the happy couple with the very packet of
tea. At one time Mazawattee had the largest wholesale tea business
in the world, but during the last war their factory in South-East
London was entirely destroyed by bombs and they are now part of a
group of food companies, still surviving, but no longer one of the
major retail tea suppliers.

Faced with this kind of marketing, the grocer gradually ceased to
blend his own tea, and was content instead to hand his customer a
packet of her favourite brand from the shelf.

By 1900 India had replaced China as the leading tea exporter,
with Ceylon not so far behind in third place. In that year exports
from China totalled 185 million pounds compared with India's
192 million pounds and Ceylon's 149 million pounds. Yet just twenty-
five years previously India had produced only 26 million pounds and
Ceylon practically none at all. From 1900 onwards China tea went
into a catastrophic decline. The early years of this century saw a
period of unrest and disturbances in China's tea-growing provinces,

culminating in the revolution of 1912 which deposed the Manchu dynasty and established a republic.

When the British abandoned Hankow the Russians took over for a time, but the demand collapsed with the Russian revolution in 1917, and the subsequent civil war. Later the Russians developed their own tea estates in the Caucasus.

Tea plantations were opened up in other parts of the world where it had been unknown before, and the British territories of Central and East Africa began to claim a share of the market. Cultivation started in Nyasaland in 1902, followed by Kenya in 1925 and subsequently Uganda and Tanganyika. Entering the tea industry at this relatively late stage, these countries were able to take advantage of all the latest technical advances in tea cultivation and processing.

Yet when all these factors have been taken into account the basic explanation for the failure of China tea in the world markets of the first half of the twentieth century is simply that the industry failed to move with the times. In China the plucking season is short, lasting only from May to July. China tea was still grown haphazardly by the peasants on their smallholdings, and could not compete with the great plantations of India and Ceylon, where large amounts of capital were invested and where the climate allowed plucking to continue for the greater part of the year with a higher financial return.

The British and Chinese tea merchants watched with concern as their flourishing businesses shrank and disappeared after more than two centuries. Supporters of China tea tried to revive the trade by criticizing the thicker-bodied and more strongly flavoured Indian teas. China teas, they contended, had little or no trace of tannin and were pleasant and refreshing to the most sensitive of constitutions, but the protests were unavailing. The fashionable put their money into British tea-plantation shares and their custom went with it. 'China or India?' was a question still asked at tea-time but in a diminishing number of high-class hotels and restaurants. The importers who had the task of filling millions of quarter-pound packets of popular Indian and Ceylon blends every year were just not interested.

In the 1930's a violent period of civil war in China, followed by the Japanese invasion, further disrupted the China tea industry, and exports fell to negligible quantities. Of course, tea was, and still is, grown by the Chinese on an enormous scale for local consumption, and some continued to be sent overland to the Soviet Union. But with the outbreak of the Second World War and with it the imposition of tea rationing in Britain, shipments of China tea stopped altogether. Six years later, at the end of the war, few remembered China tea, and fewer still cared.

After more than 250 years the China trade, the trade which had seen the East Indiamen and the clipper ships come and go, was dead at last. Or was it?

Above, Pioneer planters sitting on the verandah of a Ceylon planter's bungalow nearly a hundred years ago.

Right, The packing machine invented by John Horniman, an Isle of Wight trader who was the first man to sell tea in sealed packets in 1826.

An auction in the saleroom at East India House in 1808.

A famous Mincing Lane auction. Mr Guyowen, the auctioneer, is knocking down a parcel of Ceylon Gartmore Golden Tips to Mr Jackson, buyer for Mazawattee, for £25 10s. per pound.

The Boston Tea Party, 16th December 1773. A group of Americans, disguised as Indians, boarding the East Indiamen to throw the chests of tea into the sea.

East Indiamen anchored off Spithead.

'Going 14 knots, royal stunsails and flying kites set and wind strong from W.S.W.' *Ariel* and *Taeping* off the Lizard near the end of the Great Tea Race from China to London 1866.

Sir Lancelot, a clipper built by Robert Steele of Greenock, which made Foochow to Dungeness in a record 87 days in 1869. She foundered in a cyclone in the Bay of Bengal in 1895.

THIRD CATALOGUE

The Weights given are approximate and not guaranteed

Lot Numbers 3243 to 3258

AT THE AUCTION ROOM OF
THE TEA BROKERS' ASSOCIATION OF LONDON
PLANTATION HOUSE

CHINA BLACK TEA

FOR SALE

BY AUCTION

BY ORDER OF

THE CHINA NATIONAL TEA EXPORT CORPORATION

ON

WEDNESDAY 22nd OCTOBER, 1958

709 Packages China Tea
In Wooden Packages in Mats.

10 Large Breaks   6 Small Breaks

GOW, WILSON & STANTON, Ltd.,

(Members of the Tea Brokers' Association of London)
BROKERS,
13, ROOD LANE, E.C.3.

Telephone No.: MANsion House 3440 (7 lines)

NOTICE.—Deposits on Teas offered in this Catalogue will be charged as follows :—

Minimum Deposit £2 per package.

Price per lb.				Deposit per package.
2/– and over	...	...	...	£2
3/– ,, ,,	...	...	...	£3
4/– ,, ,,	...	...	...	£4
5/– ,, ,,	...	...	...	£5
6/– ,, ,,	...	...	...	£6
7/– ,, ,,	...	...	...	£7
8/– ,, ,,	...	...	..	£8 etc.

Smith & Ebbs, Limited, Printers, Northumberland Alley, E.C.3

Catalogue of China tea sold in the London auctions on 22nd October, 1958. The prices in handwriting are, from the left: the broker's valuation, the author's valuation, the reserve (in frame), realization price and the initials of the buying broker.

---

6   Gow, W & S, October 22, 1958

China Tea (Mint W)

JENKONG (372)

Lot	Box		lbs.
3254	1496 (5001)	90 Chs. Bro. Or. Pek.	8370 (558)

2/2   2/2   [1/10½]   2/3¼ SH.

| 3255 | 1497 (5001) | 90 Chs. Bro. Or. Pek. | 8370 (558) |

2/2   2/2   [2/1]   2/3¼ SH.

| 2256 | 1498 (5001) | 90 Chs. Bro. Or. Pek. | 8370 (558) |

2/2   2/2   [2/–]   2/3¾ SH.

| 3257 | 1499 (5002) | 54 Hf-Chs. Bro. Or. Pek. Fnngs. | 4482 (498) |

2/–   2/–   [1/9]   2/¼ SS.

| 3258 | 1500 (5002) | 48 Hf-Chs. Bro. Or. Pek. Fnngs. | 3984 (498) |

2/–   2/–   —   2/¼ SSS.

Total 709 Pkgs.

Teas being examined at the City of London Laboratories on behalf of the Port of London Health Authority.

Part of the optical equipment at the City of London Laboratories.

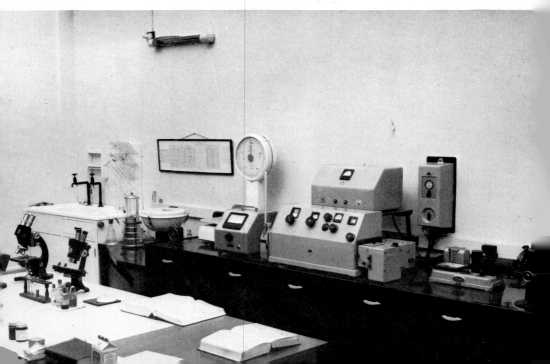

ASSAM TEA

The Dekhari Tea Company Limited.

THOWRA Inv. 78 (40)

1/2

Butler's G/Ford   Maipura 70/437

Lot	Box		Chs.	kgs.	
1	1233	40½PD	10	468	
			10	470	**42½ C**
		4064/4103	20	939	
				1877	

77

40½

41 p.

Inv. 82 (120)

2	1234	60 BP	10	488	
			10	490	
		4104/63	20	980	**41 S**
			20	980	
		41 p.		2938	

3/2

72 76

41½ 40½

3	1235	60 PF	10	488	
			10	490	
		4164/4223	20	980	**44½ C**
			20	962	
		43 p.		2920	

42½

First page of the first catalogue of tea sold at the new auction room at Sir John Lyon House, in the City, on 15th February 1971, Decimal Day.

Count Rumford's percolator—really a drip pot—invented in Paris in about 1806. The rod in the centre is a handle for the coffee compressor and the compartment encasing the pot is a hot-water jacket to keep the coffee hot.

Arab coffee pot from Mombasa with its own charcoal heater underneath.

7

The Indian Summer of China Tea

In 1950, to the surprise of all, the first shipments of China tea for eleven years reached the London market. There was not much of it, and what there was was not very good. These first post-war supplies were large-leafed teas of indifferent quality which disheartened the surviving China brokers who remembered the great days of China tea. Even in China, some primitive forms of mechanization had been introduced and now the tea was unsuitable both for the demands of the traditional China tea-drinker and for the large-scale requirements of the proprietary blended packet trade.

The manner in which it was offered was unsatisfactory too. It bore a Chinese reference number which meant nothing in Mincing Lane, and no name either of the area or of the factory by which to identify it.

In the old days the China Tea Importers' Association had been an important body. In the post-war period it barely managed to maintain its existence. Without being sure of the market, buyers bought some of these post-war teas for their China blends. Their hesitation proved justified. The new China tea just did not sell rapidly enough in the shops, even in the brighter economic climate which followed the end of tea rationing in October 1952.

The new Conservative Government was keen to dismantle the wartime apparatus of rationing, but in an orderly manner. Their Labour predecessors had de-rationed sweets too soon, with the result that the sweet-shops, with insufficient supplies, were overwhelmed by the demand and rationing had to be reimposed. The Conservatives were anxious to avoid this kind of mistake.

This time large stocks of tea were built up for some time before rationing ended, but the expected rush to buy did not materialize. So slack was the market, against all the forecasts, that many plantations, as I had known from my experience in Nyasaland, had cut back their production. Gradually the demand revived with the

growing prosperity of the 1950's, and then in 1954 came the Great
Tea Scramble.

The Indian and Ceylon governments placed an export duty on
tea, an ironic contrast to the whole history of China tea, bedevilled
for so many years by a tax on imports at the British end, and at the
same time there were some exaggerated reports that the new
season's teas would be in short supply. Rumour fed on rumour,
prices rocketed, and on the back of this seller's market even teas
from China began to find buyers, who chopped it up and included
it, in modest proportions, in some of the proprietary blends. North
Indian broken grades of average quality were fetching 6s. 10d.
(34p) per pound at the auctions, the highest figure in living
memory, and the buyers were so short of stocks that they were prepared to take anything that looked, smelt or tasted even remotely
suitable.

During this period of panic buying Sir John Kotelawala, then
Prime Minister of Ceylon, added to the excitement by publicly con-
tending that the prices which the British housewife was then paying
for tea were 'damned ridiculous'. When tea was de-rationed the controlled price was 3s. 8d. (18p) per pound. Two years later the average
price was about double that amount, so there were plenty of people
ready to lend an ear to any suggestion that the tea merchants were
profiteering.

Sir John alleged that tea was being bought by dealers at 3s. to
4s. (15–20p) per pound in Ceylon and was being sold in Britain for
7s. (35p). When the tea trade challenged Sir John to produce these
supplies at the price he had quoted he was unable to do so. Subsequently he retracted his allegations. It turned out that dealers were
in fact paying 5s. (25p) per pound in Ceylon and that to this figure
had to be added the Ceylon Government's export duty of 1s. 11½d.
(10p). The publicity given to Sir John's remarks, unjustified though
they were, proved to be the turning point. Certain of the leading
firms introduced new, cheaper blends. In various parts of the
country a buyers' strike developed. Housewives cut down their
purchases of tea, waiting for the price to fall.

Finally, on 16th February 1955, a day which has become known
in the trade as 'Wild Wednesday', the bottom suddenly fell out of
the market. Throughout the day there were sensational price move-
ments, 'the like of which', wrote a trade writer at the time, 'have not
been witnessed on this or any other market in the history of the
commodity'. At the lowest point, teas were being sold at 2s. (10p) and
even 3s. (15p) per pound less than they had been fetching only a day
or two previously. Before the day was out, the suppliers began to

withhold teas from the auctions. Bidding became more animated, and prices started to recover. But never since have they reached the levels prevailing just prior to 'Wild Wednesday'.

With the market stabilized, the temporary demand for China tea disappeared and for the twelve months before I joined my new employers in June 1956 the company, as agents for the Chinese, had made no sales. The Chinese Tea Corporation in Peking wanted to know why their teas were not selling and what should be done to make them sell. My job would be to advise them.

For my first venture into market research I set out to meet the old China brokers. I found three of them still making part of their living from occasional shipments of China tea which reached England from Formosa and Hong Kong. One of them had been born in China, and as a boy had survived the Boxer rebellion. His father had watched the tall ships set out on the great tea races. These old brokers were only too pleased to talk of the past, and from them I gained some first-hand impressions of the great days of China tea. I was glad I took the opportunity of doing so, for within the next few years all three had died. Their deaths meant that there was hardly anybody left with an expert knowledge of what the classic China teas had really tasted like in the days before 1914, when the China trade had still been large enough to command respect and the hundreds of individual teas selling under mark names had not been reduced to a few broad types.

But their reminiscences, fascinating as they were, seemed to be of little use for the job in hand, so I asked all the major firms of blenders and packers for their opinions of China tea. I found that the market for the traditional leaf grades of China tea, the Lapsang souchong, the Keemun and the exotic scented and flavoured teas, was so limited that the blenders and wholesalers could hardly take their prospects seriously. The only people who bought them, and who could afford to pay the prices asked, which were much higher than those of proprietary blends, were a diminishing number of old ladies in Cheltenham and Chelsea who remembered China tea from their youth.

To talk about 'China tea' in a general way is almost as meaningless as talking about 'French wine' in a general way. Years ago there were hundreds of quite separate growing districts, each producing its own characteristic tea, crack marks or chops, as they were called, but since World War II there have been only four main China teas left.

Lapsang souchong, the most celebrated and nostalgic, is the large-leaf congou black tea with the tarry flavour got from its being

smoked over a charcoal fire. It comes from South China. Keemun
was originally a green tea, which in the early 1880's started to be
manufactured as black tea. It was a North China congou described
as having a thick, full liquor and rich aroma, and today is the most
widely sold of the China teas. Caper tea, a rarity on the British
market, is black tea rolled into little balls like capers.

Jasmine tea is green tea which has had dried flowers added to it.
It is the last survivor of a range of flower-flavoured teas. Gunpowder
is another green tea, but a rarity like caper tea and rolled into small
balls in the same way.

Earl Grey used to be a China blend for which Jackson's of
Piccadilly held the original recipe, but other firms followed with
their own Earl Grey blends and with the break in supplies of oriental
teas during the 1939–45 war other forms of artificial flavouring were
used, the principal one being bergamot oil.

None of these teas appealed to me as tea I would want to drink
at home, since I had been trained to appreciate the merits of orthodox
modern teas from Darjeeling, Assam and Ceylon.

I became convinced that the only sound commercial future for
China tea lay in their producing a machine-made blending-type
tea, suitable for inclusion with others in the British proprietary blends,
and this was essentially a manufacturing rather than a marketing
problem. When I discussed this with my English buying acquaintan-
ces their reaction was not encouraging. From their pre-war days
the senior blenders could remember the scented, weedy taste of
China teas and they were quite firm that they wanted no such taste
in their blends. All this had to be conveyed to Peking and explained
to the Chinese representative in London, Liao Run-chu, of the
Commercial Counsellor's office.

Liao had come to England with the Trade Mission as a sort of
Mandarin without Portfolio and there he found himself assigned to
promoting the tea trade. He was very much a product of modern
China, a sound, orthodox Maoist supporter, probably under thirty
and undoubtedly a former soldier in Mao's army. He was tough and
he was intelligent. He knew no English at all. My negotiations with
him had to be carried on against a background of furiously antago-
nistic politics and propaganda, although politics were never brought
into our discussions, and the Chinese never showed any personal
animosity whatever. There was, of course, a long and daunting
history of bad relations between our countries.

For thousands of years the Chinese had developed their civilization in almost total isolation. Not only were they certain of their
innate superiority over other races, but their rulers preferred not to

have their people contaminated by foreign ideas. However, by the nineteenth century the world hunger for trade could be held in check no longer. The riches of China tempted the European nations and the Japanese, who between them put China at gun point, seized much of her outlying territories and forced her to open 'treaty ports' to their merchants. The Chinese had always spoken of outsiders as *yang kuei-tzu*, or 'foreign devils', and in a short time their age-old prejudice turned to informed dislike. Powerless to resist the guns and with no redress against dishonest treaties, they made themselves as unwelcoming as they could, to the extent of cutting off the heads of many missionaries and not a few sailors on shore leave and inquisitive travellers who penetrated into the interior.

The merchants were greedy and often not too scrupulous in their transactions. They were backed by foreign armies and supported by local Chinese bureaucracy, also hated by the Chinese people because it enforced the authority of the Manchus, themselves regarded as foreigners from the north, although they had ruled China for 300 years.

Ruling the Celestial Kingdom was the sinister old Empress Dowager, the effective head of the disintegrating Manchu Dynasty. She feared and hated the foreign powers even more than her predecessors. By the end of the nineteenth century China had been divided up by the Western nations, Japan and Russia into 'spheres of influence', and Britain, who had the largest sphere of influence, had appriopriated the huge black-tea-growing area of the Yangtze Provinces as her special interest. China was becoming like Africa, an area to be colonized, but the Empress saw an opportunity to put an end to this humiliating state of affairs.

In 1900 a fanatical group of militant anti-foreigners called the Boxers were egged on by her to attempt a massacre of the foreigners living in the Legation Quarter of Peking. The attempt narrowly failed, and was nearly the end of the Celestial Empress herself, but it brought home to the eleven occupying powers how unpopular they were, and their influence in their respective spheres was never so great again. China fell into confusion, bedevilled by foreign wars and internal strife from which she did not emerge until the New Regime in 1950, which swept away not only the trappings of the Celestial Kingdom but also the concessions of the predatory foreigners.

After the Opium Wars in 1842 it would have seemed ridiculous to doubt that China must give up her isolation because of the sheer pressure of the march of history. Even though the outsiders forced her to open her frontiers by the most blameworthy methods, China could not for ever be a forbidden empire of several hundred million people. Yet not much more than a century from the start of this trade by force China has managed to regain all her isolation which she kept inviolate for 3,000 years. Apart from a few people who are permitted to visit China because the People's Republic may have some use for them, foreigners are few, restricted and not wholly welcome.

There was certainly no established tradition of international friendship to build on. I soon found that there was no common professional experience either. Liao knew nothing about tea!

All discussions took place through an interpreter at first, but there were inevitably difficulties about the terms used in tea-tasting. I also had to teach Liao to taste in the English fashion, with milk. At the same time, I had sent a lot of samples to China to inform the Tea Corporation of the standards expected on the London market. Strange as the post-war China teas were to the London brokers and buyers, the British blends must have been even stranger to the Chinese tea experts, who had been isolated from the rest of the world for years and had in any case never regarded other countries' tea with much interest. The high quality of the Indian and Ceylon teas dismayed them as, so far as I could discover, their rolling machines were of wood and hand-operated, vastly different from the modern plant used in Ceylon and India. However, they studied my tasting reports and gave careful consideration to all my suggestions. They asked for detailed information about processing plant used in other parts of the world.

Any decision to modernize, even small selected areas, would be an important one. For the Chinese to evolve a strain of tea plant, possibly an Assam hybrid, and manufacture tea comparable to the tea which the British public was used to, was a horticultural and technical problem which could take years to solve. The Chinese had to be convinced that it was worth while to compete for a share, possibly only a small share, in the British market when they already had a home market of 700 million people who were satisfied with China tea as it was.

By 1958 the Chinese were producing a low-priced, low-grade, but not unacceptable tea which I was able to sell for them to one or two large blenders 'for shipment', which meant that if the buyer liked the sample he would place a contract for say, 2,000 chests to be shipped from Shanghai.

This was success of a kind, but these direct contracts were negotiated outside the main Mincing Lane market, and I was convinced that if China tea was ever to take its place beside Indian and Ceylon and African tea it would have to be offered for sale in the weekly auctions and make its way in straightforward competition.

By this time an English-speaking tea expert had been sent out from Peking, and although the whole capitalist system, epitomized by the City of London, was anathema to them, the Chinese agreed to produce a selection of new, manufactured tea for the auctions. As soon as the London tea trade heard about this, rumours started that the Chinese were about to flood the market with cheap tea. The Chinese reacted angrily to this and replied that they had no intention of exploiting their people or allowing them to be exploited to provide the British with cheap tea, and in any case they could not supply more than 10 million pounds of tea a year, compared with total imports into this country of 558 million pounds.

On Wednesday, 22nd October 1958, 300 years after China tea had first been drunk in this country, and twenty years after its last appearance in the auctions, China tea came under the hammer in Mincing Lane before a crowded auditorium. It was offered on behalf of the Tea Corporation of the People's Republic of China and it was the first time the Chinese producers had put their tea in the London auctions themselves.

The prices fetched were modest enough, but the 'blending-type' teas which I had been campaigning for sold best and the first step had been taken towards making China tea a respectable, orthodox tea. Weekly auctions of Chinas continued until February 1959, by which time 10,248 chests had been offered. The total realised was £73,823, the average selling price being slightly over 2s. (10p) per pound.

Shortly afterwards I joined an old-established tea brokerage firm in Mincing Lane, which meant that my Chinese principals would have the same broker's services as all the other producing companies. Gradually I found China blending teas becoming accepted as one major blending company after another found that the new tea was suitable for them. In July 1960 the *Tea and Rubber Mail* printed an article of mine under the heading 'China teas find increasing acceptance for British proprietary blends', a great contrast with the unfavourable publicity of less than two years before.

Then I heard ominous news that some China teas, though not my contracts, had been forbidden to land because of excess lead content. New 'Lead in Food' regulations had been announced, and the Port of London Health Authority had started systematic tests. The excess found was usually minimal and only a small number of samples was affected, but advice was given to the blending companies not to include more than a given proportion of certain tea in their blends. Then the real blow fell. A consignment of tea from Formosa was condemned by the Health Authorities.

Almost overnight the demand for China tea vanished. No tea buyer would take a chance on 'buying forward' if the consignment might not be allowed into the country when it arrived and no tea company would risk being connected with a contaminated tea. My job for the Chinese Tea Corporation became impossible for the time being, although some importers who still dealt in tea in the old way managed to buy a little by private contracts in China, using their agents' information on which teas to avoid because of likely trouble.* For more than five years I had worked with Liao and his colleagues, Chang Chi-cheng and Wang Ping-yu, and I took my leave of them with sincere regret.

A few months after this China invaded Tibet and even threatened the tea estates in the extreme north of India. The political climate between Britain and China deteriorated rapidly and many of the Chinese diplomatic personnel were changed. China tea imports for 1962 only reached 30,000 chests and in no year since have they reached more than two-thirds of their peak of 116,000 chests in 1960, while tea from such a new producing country as Uganda has multiplied three times. It is obvious that official policy in Peking is no longer enthusiastically supporting this part of their export trade, and, instead, China tea is being sent to countries where political ties are strong and her traditional manufacturing methods still acceptable. Egypt and Morocco are her biggest buyers. As years go on and African countries in particular steadily improve their teas, China must find it more and more difficult to compete in a market where the future is uncertain even for established teas.

* Possible causes of the lead contamination could have been: chemical sprays; dilapidated lead paint in some factory, or the use of solder for repairing worn machinery. Although the precise source was never revealed, it must have been discovered and rectified because in 1964, Dr. Amphlett Williams, public analyst to the City and Port of London Health Authorities, reported that no samples showed more than the permitted limit of ten parts of lead per mil.

8

*The Evolution of Tea-
and Coffee-brewing*

It took me a little time to catch my breath after ending my association with the Chinese, but soon I was looking for another way of involving myself in tea and coffee.

I learnt that a tea and coffee company were looking for someone to start a branch for them on the South Coast, selling mainly to the catering and restaurant trade. The one aspect of tea and coffee that I had as yet no knowledge of was the business of selling it to the people who served it to the public, but I was sure it could not be as difficult as selling a not very good tea to professional tea buyers who did not really want it, so I applied for the job and got it.

From working with people who knew their tea and coffee backwards and who all spoke the same language—even, eventually, the Chinese—I found myself in the big outside world where most people know very little about tea but they do know what they like. I also became acquainted with tea- and coffee-brewing machines, a subject which was to claim more and more of my attention as time went on. It was obvious that a small tea and coffee firm would not necessarily choose to compete with the proprietary quarter-pound-packet business and therefore they concentrated on supplying bulk users such as the hotels and restaurants.

The history of coffee-brewing equipment is longer and more complex than is generally realized and it goes back into the eighteenth century. Over the past 200 years an amazing amount of effort and ingenuity have been put into the search for the perfect coffee-making machine. But to put the story into its proper context it may be helpful first to review the methods by which coffee was made in early times.

In Ethiopia, more than a thousand years ago, coffee was regarded as a food, not a drink. The berries, beans and hulls were all crushed and mixed with fat into food-balls, a useful supply of nourishment to take on long journeys through the mountains. It was only in about the year 1300 that coffee was first used as a beverage. Unfortunately, the food value of coffee, its protein and fat content, is wasted in the way we use it, the only constituents which we absorb being those which are soluble in hot water. When coffee is correctly made the hot water is in contact with the ground coffee for only a few minutes, so that the bulk of the protein, which forms up to 15% and is almost insoluble, remains in the grounds which are thrown away.

In the tenth century, which was early days for coffee, a kind of wine was made from the fermented pulp of the ripe berries. The beans and hulls were simply crushed, and cold water added. The idea of boiling coffee to make a refreshing drink came about a century later, but even then the beans were not roasted. That development did not occur for another 200 years. Then someone had the bright idea of pounding the roasted beans into a powder by means of a mortar and pestle. The drink was made by casting a quantity of the powder into boiling water, and it was swallowed complete with the grounds.

As coffee spread to the Levant, the system was to steep the powder in water for a day, then boil the liquor half-away, strain it, and keep it in earthenware jars until required.

By the sixteenth century the appearance of a small coffee boiler helped to speed up the process. While the brew was boiling, cinnamon and cloves would sometimes be added, and after the coffee had been poured out into small cups a drop of essence of amber would complete the drink. Later on the primitive coffee boiler was provided with a cover and so became the forerunner of the modern coffee-pot.

In oriental countries it became the custom to pour boiling water directly on to powdered coffee in the cup. Infusion came in during the eighteenth century; ground coffee was placed in a cloth bag in the pot, and hot water poured on, the brew then being allowed to infuse, just like tea. Boiling, however, continued to be the favourite method of preparing the beverage for many years. In a rare book published in London in 1662 appears the following recipe which describes how coffee was made in the seventeenth century and which makes it easy to understand why tea, without coffee's roasting problems, became so popular.

To make the drink that is now much used called coffee

The coffee-berries are to be bought at any Druggist, about three shillings the pound; Take what quantity you please, and over a charcoal fire, in an old pudding-pan or frying-pan, keep them always stirring until they be quite black, and when you crack one with your teeth that it is black within as it is without; yet if you exceed, then do you waste the Oyl, which only makes the drink; and if less, then will it not deliver its Oyl, which makes the drink; and if you should continue fire till it be white, it will then make no coffee, but only give you its salt. The Berry prepared as above, beaten and forced through a Lawn Sive, is then fit for use.

Take clean water, and boil one-third of it away what quantity soever it be, and it is fit for use. Take one quart of this prepared Water, put in it one ounce of your prepared coffee, and boil it gently one-quarter of an hour, and it is fit for your use; drink one-quarter of a pint as hot as you can sip it.

Coffee in those days seems to have been very similar to what most Englishmen imagine to be modern Turkish coffee—which is a very strong and syrupy brew made from very finely ground beans.

For the first time the muslin sieve had been introduced for filtering coffee, and this may have brought about the idea that good coffee was better made by infusion rather than boiling. From the description quoted, however, it is apparent that instant coffee was still a long way off in 1662, and it is not surprising that inventors soon turned their attention to devising some simpler and quicker method.

Coffee-making devices can be divided into several main groups. To the simple boiling and infusing pots of early times can be added the percolators, vacuum and filter machines, and in more recent years the dispensing and vending machines, the latter two forming a whole new industry of their own, facilitating push-button sales not only of coffee and tea but of other commodities too.

Percolation, strictly speaking, means allowing hot water to pass through the ground coffee once only, and then through small holes in the container (usually of china or metal) and into the coffee-pot beneath. The filter method, in contrast, means passing the hot water through a porous material, usually cloth or paper, which holds the water in contact with the coffee for a longer time.

The first percolator appears to have been invented by Jean Baptiste de Belloy, who was Archbishop of Paris and who liked visiting the coffee houses of the city. His device was first used in about 1800. The ground coffee was held in a perforated metal container in the top and hot water was poured into it.

Six years later Benjamin Thompson, an Anglo-American scientist who was also known as Count Rumford, invented an improved percolator in which a ramming device was used to spread and compress the ground coffee evenly in the percolating container. Count Rumford, incidentally, was one of the first to advocate adding cream and sugar to coffee. Some people put brown sugar in their coffee to give it a slightly different character, but personally I prefer the character to be in the coffee rather than the sugar.

The principles of de Belloy's and Count Rumford's percolators are still used in modern coffee-making appliances, but it will be seen that many of our domestic coffee-makers described as percolators at the present time are not true percolators because they use steam pressure to raise hot water up through a central tube and spray it continuously over and over again through the ground coffee. This type of machine, the origins of which go back to the early nineteenth century, is known as the pumping percolator. When people say that they do not like percolated coffee it is usually this method that they mean. There is certainly nothing wrong with a simple pour-over system which allows the water to drip through the coffee and then through a strainer or a filter.

Around 1817, earthenware pots, fitted at first with a strainer at the top rather like the early French percolators, became popular for making coffee in England. Later on the strainer was replaced by a bag of flannel or muslin, suspended from the rim. The bag held the ground coffee, and the water was poured into and through it. This type became known as the coffee biggin, and is the ancestor of the modern filter machine.

The next development of consequence was the appearance of the first vacuum-operated machine, invented in 1840 by Robert Napier, the celebrated Scottish marine engineer. To us it is an extraordinary device, a complicated piece of machinery worthy almost of an Emmet or a Heath Robinson. It consisted of a silver globe with a brewing syphon and a strainer, the heat source being either gas or spirits. First, a small amount of water had to be placed in the globe before the gas or wick was lit. Ground coffee was put in the receiver, which then had to be filled with boiling water. In due course clear coffee was syphoned over into the globe, passing through a tube fitted with a strainer to which was added a filter cloth. The Napier machine, for all its complication, still required a separate source of boiling water; it did not boil its own. Nevertheless, it is of some interest because this machine provided the inspiration for a number of variations in larger steam coffee machines for use in hotels and restaurants and on board ship.

Also from the 1840's originates the type of machine using two glass bowls, the coffee being filtered from one into the other. This method was revived in America at the time of the First World War, and in a modernized form and with many improvements the same principle is used today in the Cona and Cory machines.

Before the Industrial Revolution the need to make tea or coffee quickly and in large quantities did not exist, but the nineteenth century saw for the first time the phenomenon of large numbers of men working together in factories. With the growth of the towns and improvements in transport they were obliged to live further and further away from their work. Working hours were long, and so it became necessary for employers to provide some sort of refreshment. From these origins developed the modern mass catering industry that we know today, and with it the whole range of specialised equipment used by present-day caterers.

In a previous chapter I have explained how, with the decline of the eighteenth-century coffee houses, tea established itself as the national drink in British homes. It is possible that coffee-drinking might have disappeared altogether if it had not been for the arrival on the industrial scene of the first caterers. Workers might drink tea at home—partly, no doubt, at their wives' insistence—but at work they often drank coffee. An important factor in this trend was the great temperance crusade.

In the first half of the nineteenth century drunkenness was a considerable and growing social evil in Britain. Huge new industries were springing up, and all too often the only place of refreshment available to the workers was the public house, then quite unhampered by the restrictions of modern licensing hours.

As far back as 1843 John Wesley urged his followers to abstain from alcohol, and the evangelical movement came to the forefront of the temperance campaign. Temperance societies flourished up and down the country, followed by the formation in 1856 of the National Temperance League. Perhaps their most dramatic success was the 'blue-ribbon' movement, which meant that those who had signed the pledge agreed to wear a blue ribbon as a sign of their total abstinence.

These earnest temperance enthusiasts quickly appreciated the need for something non-alcoholic for the labouring classes to drink. A series of 'British Workman' establishments sprang up imitating the public house in appearance but without the strong drink. There were 'coffee palaces' and 'coffee taverns'. They sold tea as well as coffee, but they kept the taste for coffee alive. Then there were the 'People's Cafés', under the presidency of Lord Shaftesbury, the famous reformer who supported temperance (in the correct sense of the word) but was not a total abstainer. These started in 1874 and were the forerunners of our modern chains of tea shops.

About this time John Pearce in London was running his 'Gutter Hotel', a pioneer mobile canteen, and supplying tea, coffee and other refreshments at low prices. In the next decade he opened a dining room which he called *Pearce and Plenty*, where before long he was serving 3,000 meals a day between 12 noon and 3 p.m. *Pearce and Plenty* proved to be the first of a chain of similar restaurants which lasted into the twentieth century and were eventually taken over by the Aerated Bread Co., better known as the A.B.C. cake shops and cafés. For the first time mass catering outside the licensed trade had arrived as a new kind of service to the public, and as a new way of making a living. It was in fact the A.B.C. which started the tea shop as we now know it.

The building of the railways brought travel within the reach of the ordinary people for the first time. During a long and tiring journey the passengers wanted something to eat and drink, so the railway-station refreshment room, butt of music-hall comedians from that day to this, came into being, giving a further impetus to the new catering industry.

All these catering establishments needed some method of making coffee and tea, lots of it, at short notice, and enterprising people in several countries tried to supply the deficiency. So appeared the first of those hissing, steaming monsters that have baffled generations of travellers but are known in the catering trade as café sets. Americans, Frenchmen, Italians and Englishmen all helped to pioneer the making of coffee in bulk.

As early as 1843 a French inventor was working on a large-scale hydrostatic percolator which came into its own in the Exposition of 1855, when it was said that 2,000 cups of coffee were made in an hour. It should be admitted, however, that these were probably very small cups, *demi-tasses*. The Italians improved on this with their rapid filter machines, which were prominent by the turn of the century. Some had a curiously octopus-like appearance, but they could produce as many as 1,500 cups of coffee an hour.

In 1902 W. M. Still and Sons of London, famous to this day as manufacturers of catering equipment, were granted an English patent for a steam coffee-making machine using 12 oz. of coffee to the gallon. In 1920 a Chicago inventor produced a device for use in hotels and restaurants involving perforated baskets designed to rest in a coffee urn, but which could be lifted out as the hot water percolated through. It was a useful improvement, but the principle was far from new.

In the following year, in Cleveland, a rapid infuser came out, designed to make an extract in only thirty-eight seconds and to deliver a gallon of concentrated coffee essence every three minutes. A dispenser was fitted to this machine, automatically regulating the quantity of coffee base added to boiling water, and capable of serving 600 cups per hour.

It seems that coffee has always had a strange but potent appeal to those with an inventive turn of mind. Between 1789 and 1921 the United States Patent Office alone recorded more than 800 devices for brewing coffee, not to mention 185 for grinders, 312 for roasters and 175 miscellaneous inventions with some bearing on coffee.

While coffee was being subjected to all these forms of physical violence, tea maintained its popularity in British homes, where its method of preparation was by comparison blessedly simple. However, several people applied themselves to the problem of making the brewing of tea more complicated, and the first teapot patent was issued in 1774 to John Wadham, who devised a 'tea fountain' which added little to the conventional teapot except that it included a rod of cast iron down the middle which was heated and intended to keep the tea hot. This was followed by patents for tea urns which were heated by spirit lamps, and in 1812 Mrs. Sarah Guppy patented a teapot with a wire basket in it for boiling eggs! Later in the century there was a vogue for perforated metal containers or linen bags to hold the tea in the teapot, and this naturally led to tea percolators and infusers, but none of these ideas supplanted the simple teapot which for an ordinary family or small party could not really be improved upon.

However, when it became necessary to cater for large numbers of people, urns and boilers had to be used and the earliest and simplest of these, with its cylindrical boiler and muslin tea bag, is still familiar to day in church halls and at garden fêtes. In restaurants and other places where something more sophisticated is used the machines are still designed only to heat the water, since the only satisfactory method of making tea is still to pour freshly boiling water on to the tea leaves.

I soon became very familiar with catering equipment, since it was the all-important link between the tea and coffee that I was selling and the tea and coffee which the public drink. Most of the machines did their job admirably, but inexpert handling or lack of proper maintenance could cause them to produce something quite undrinkable, and the tendency seemed to be to blame the tea and coffee supplier first.

As time went on I thought of more and more things I would have

liked to change. The temptation to meddle in other people's jobs
in an effort to get the kind of tea and coffee that I wanted to sell was
strong, and since I was a newcomer my suggestions were hardly
likely to be always welcome. Eventually I realised that if I wanted
to avoid upsetting people and still get things done in my own way
I would have to start a business of my own, and so in the middle of
1966 I resigned to set about forming my own company and installed
myself in an office in Royal Mail House, Southampton, just opposite
the old South Western Hotel.

Since I was intending to trade under my own name, one of the
first things I decided to do was to apply for the name Bramah to
be registered as a trade mark. All my life I had never had any trouble
with my name except the occasional difficulties with misspellings
and mispronunciations, and I expected no trouble now, but I was
wrong.

The Bramahs of Yorkshire have been spelling their name that
way for more than 200 years and were tenant farmers living in a
village just outside Barnsley as far back as the reign of Queen Anne.
One of them, Joseph Bramah, went to London in 1773 and after
working for a few years as a cabinet-maker invented and patented
the first effective thief-proof lock. This was so successful that Joseph
gave up his cabinet-making business in St. Giles and devoted himself
to his inventions, becoming one of the most versatile mechanical
engineers of his time, particularly in the field of hydraulics, and
some of his original presses are now in the Science Museum in
South Kensington. He became famous for meticulous workmanship, and the expression 'It's a Bramah' is still used by crafts-
men in some parts of the country when they mean a fine piece of
work.

His sons who carried on the business after him were steam engineers and in 1821 built and road-tested a steam-driven barouche
with the first-ever change-speed gears. A disastrous fire in 1850
destroyed the factory in Pimlico, but the Bramah Lock Company
was saved and is in business to this day. The Ernest Bramah who
wrote the Kai Lung stories was probably a relation through his
mother, whose maiden name was Bramah.

I had always been brought up to be rather proud of my name,
but the Registrar of Trade Marks did not like it. It was, the Hearing
Officer said, too close to the descriptive Indian word Brahma,
meaning 'supreme god', and might cause offence to the adherents
of the Hindu religion living in this country. This surprised me,
since I had met many Indians of the highest caste during my career,
and none of them had ever shown any sign of being offended

Early coffee syphon invented by Robert Napier, a distinguished marine engineer.

A superb silver-plated coffee syphon machine made in Sheffield in about 1860.

A syphon machine incorporating a balance which enables the flame to be extinguished when the process of making the coffee reaches the correct stage.

A match-striking alarm tea maker of about 1900; forerunner of the
modern electric tea makers.

An internally heated hot water urn, usually known as a samovar.

Early Cona machine which makes coffee by the vacuum method.

Below, Porcelain coffee percolator in the form of an early French locomotive, with gilt metal undercarriage and wheels and fired by a spirit lamp. The ground coffee was placed in a basket in the funnel. This coffee maker was sold at Sotheby's in 1970 for £800.

Examples of domestic filter pots which make excellent coffee by a very simple method.

The Bramah filter machine which can make three pints of fresh coffee every three or four minutes, and only takes ten seconds to operate.

Above, The paper used for making filter papers being examined in a Northumberland paper mill.

Left, The first commercial automatic all electric 'teas-made', invented by W. H. Brenner Thornton in 1932.

by my name, nor shown any curiosity as to how I got it. The patent agents, on my behalf, argued that although Brahma may indeed mean 'supreme god', and also for that matter a breed of cattle and a type of domestic fowl, it was still not the same as Bramah, which, however unusual, was a long-established surname.

The Office of the Indian High Commission was consulted and a letter was received from the librarian which started by correcting our assumption that Bramah was a transliteration of Brahma; in fact Brahma was a transliteration of a Sanskrit word written in the Devanagari script. It was admitted that to a well-educated Indian the word Bramah would have no meaning, but less well educated Indians, not so familiar with the niceties of correct transliteration, could regard it as an anglicized or Europeanized version of Brahma, for the two words would sound the same when pronounced by a European.

This excursion into the realms of hypothesis completely bewildered me since there seemed no limit to the possible misunderstandings of an ill-educated foreigner living in a country whose language he did not speak very well. The Registrar of Companies had raised no objection on these grounds when I registered my company, and indeed could hardly have done so since other members of the family in Yorkshire already had companies in existence including the 200-year-old Bramah Lock Co. I then learnt from my patent agents that there was another group of people who could be offended, those who lived in this country and had adopted the Hindu religion but were not of Indian origin themselves. It was proposed that the matter should be referred to the Registrar of Trade Marks in India for his ruling.

I could see that before much longer I should feel like an undesirable alien in the country my ancestors had lived in for hundreds of years, so I decided to write to a brilliant and resourceful Indian friend who knew many people at the Indian High Commission. I hoped she could find a short cut to someone of authority who could give me a favourable decision before I became enmeshed in the toils of the Indian Civil Service. She was astonished to hear of the Registrar of Trade Marks' objections, and obtained a personal letter from the Acting High Commissioner stating that the *Trade Marks Journal of India* included several names of Indian gods which had been registered as trade marks, and he could see no reason why Bramah as a trade mark should cause any offence.

My appeal against the original rejection of my application was granted and upheld. The application was published in the *Trade*

Marks Journal for three consecutive months and objections were awaited. There were no objections. Bramah became Registered Trade Mark 898,576.

My first move after taking possession of my office was to enlarge my study of the various kinds of tea- and coffee-brewing machines. This seemed to me absolutely vital, for I wanted to provide a complete service for tea and coffee consumers and this meant preparing my own blends of both coffee and tea which would be most suitable for the differing types of equipment.

It was my personal experience in my own office that turned my attention to the problems of preparing tea and coffee economically. I found that the vending machine was too large for the smaller office, while the table-top dispensing machines, using powdered ingredients, were not to everyone's taste. As I was running a tea and coffee business it was obviously essential to serve visitors with a good-quality traditional tea or coffee, and this, I discovered, was not so easy.

In those early weeks when tea was required my secretary had to walk along the corridor, fill the electric kettle, wait for it to boil, heat the teapot, make the tea and wait for it to infuse. Then, at the right moment, she or I (provided that neither of us was too busy) had to pour it out. Later still, there was the washing-up to be done. Many was the time, after a day's work, that we found we had missed afternoon tea altogether—which seemed a poor advertisement for a tea and coffee company. Often, too, I found I was making the tea myself when my secretary was occupied with the telephone or typing something important. Her time and mine, I felt, were too valuable to be wasted in this ritual.

Obviously there were thousands of other offices where time was being similarly wasted every working day. The demands of a new business prevented me from developing the idea of producing a machine straight away, but slowly, after making hundreds of sketches and dozens of models, my own machine was developed. It worked by filtering water through coffee. There is nothing new about this, but what was relatively new was the reservoir of ready-heated water which started the cycle of events. Three pints of cold water poured into the top of the machine displaced three pints of heated water which sprayed over the ground coffee held in a filter paper and funnel below. The coffee filtered into a flask within four minutes with a hot plate to keep the fresh coffee at the correct temperature. Meanwhile the three pints of cold water were heated to a thermostatically controlled temperature ready to make more coffee. The machine also made fresh, real tea. It is too long a story to tell here how one builds a machine, but it was hard work and there were many setbacks, frustrations and revisions before I could add my application to the hundreds already filed at the Patent Office. My machine belonged to the main-stream development of equipment for making ground coffee, and was not a vending machine, which works on a different principle and has a history all of its own.

9
The Vending Revolution

The vending machine belongs to the shining new world of automation, a world so new that at the beginning of the 1960's the promise and the problems affected hardly anybody. Yet the principle of automatic vending, that is the issuing of a measured quantity of something by means of a coin-operated mechanism, has a venerable history going back to classical times.

In 215 B.C. a mathematician named Hero, who lived in Alexandria, wrote a book describing a number of inventions, and one of these was an automatic coin-operated device for dispensing sacrificial water in Egyptian temples. The coin which set off the mechanism was a five-drachma piece (worth today about 30p), which seems a good deal to pay for water, and since the market for such a vending machine was necessarily limited, the invention seems to have languished for want of patrons and for centuries was completely forgotten until in 1587 Hero's *Pneumatika* was translated into Italian with illustrations. It is possible that in its new form it struck some sympathetic chord, since at the beginning of the eighteenth-century tobacco and snuff vendors appeared in English taverns and enjoyed a few years' vogue. These tobacco and snuff vendors were made of polished brass and a halfpenny inserted in the top flipped a trigger and opened the lid. The customer helped himself and the barmaid or landlord then shut the lid, so in fact the device was not fully automatic and omitted the important principle that the machine delivers a standard amount of the commodity being sold.

The search for the perfect use for a vending machine had begun, but it was not for another hundred years that it made its next appeal to the imaginations of lovers of the ingenious and the bizarre. One of the first men to see the possibilities in automatic vending was Richard Carlile, a free thinker and bookseller who had been in trouble with the police for publishing such books as Thomas Paine's *The Age of Reason*. In 1822 he decided to sell books by machine, arguing that a machine could not be prosecuted. 'My publications are sold by clockwork!' he wrote in his newspaper. 'In the shop is the dial on which is written every publication for sale. The purchaser enters and turns the hand on the dial to the publication he wants, when, on depositing his money, the publication drops down before him.' It was a good idea, but the authorities held Carlile responsible just the same and convicted one of his employees of selling blasphemous literature through his machine.

Then in 1857 Simeon Denham was issued with a British patent for a vending machine, the first automatic selling device covered by patent law. The Denham machine was a postage-stamp vendor, and so familiar is the idea today that it is surprising to find that the original machine was too clumsy to be practical and in fact it was another thirty years before inventors had solved most of the problems and fifty years before the American postal authorities started printing stamps in convenient strips which could be coiled inside the machines.

The next vending machines were those traditionally associated with railway stations and they sold cigarettes, chewing gum and chocolate. A good deal of pioneering work in this field was done in England, the Scandinavian countries, France and Germany. The German inventor Carl Ade was one of the first with a machine which sold handkerchiefs, cigarettes and sweets as far back as 1867. In 1885 a group of New York business men introduced the penny weighing machine to the United States. It was a massive machine, itself weighing around 600 lb., and it was the forerunner of countless more manageable machines which soon appeared everywhere to tell an anxious public whether it was getting fatter.

One of the English inventors was Percival Everitte, whose machine for selling postcards and writing paper appeared on Mansion House Station in 1883. In his patent application Everitte said, 'It has been found in practice that although the apparatus is perfectly successful when not designedly misused, articles such as paper, orange-peel and other rubbish have been maliciously placed in the slit provided for the admission of the coin, and that in consequence the channel provided for the passage of the coins from the slit became blocked.' For many years the temptation to sabotage the machines proved almost irresistible to the public and inventors were constantly grappling with the technical problems created by people who insisted on trying to get their chocolate for nothing by using coins attached to pieces of string which they could then retrieve.

The first real breakthrough in vending machines came when the initiative passed from the inventors of machines to the men with something they wanted to sell. In 1888 Thomas Adams, founder of the Adams Gum Company, had machines designed to sell his Tutti-Frutti gum on New York City's elevated platforms. These machines were an instant success and proved a godsend to other American gum manufacturers, who were quick to follow Adams' example. Meanwhile in England the British Automatic Company, who claim to be Britain's oldest vending company, had a machine working in 1885. It was a chicken-shaped machine which sold metal eggs with a trinket inside, all for a penny.

It was a charitable organization, oddly enough, which introduced the vending machine to France. In 1889 the Society of Stores for the Blind put ten-centime chocolate and bon-bon machines on the platforms of railway stations on the Paris to Marseilles line and they too were a success. A year later in Paris hot-water vending machines were set up at street corners so that cab drivers could get nine quarts of hot water to fill foot-warmers for their passengers. Local residents used these hot-water vendors too for supplies for their homes.

Hot-drink vending also started from a rather similar idea patented in London in 1895 by a solicitor named Robinson. He used the waste heat from street gas lamps to provide hot water and drinks. A spiral coil and superheater were fitted about a foot above the gas flame and, by the generation of steam, a reservoir of water in the base of the lamps was raised to boiling point. A halfpenny in the slot brought a gallon of hot water, and later modifications were made so as to provide a range of popular hot drinks.

There is no doubt that the idea was successful because local refreshment houses objected to 'unfair competition'. It was estimated that if only a fraction of London's street lamps were equipped, 120 million gallons of hot water could be produced each year at $\frac{1}{2}$d. a gallon. In 1898 at the south-east corner of Leicester Square an elaborate lamp was erected to provide not only hot water but cocoa, coffee and beef tea. The demand was so great that the lamp was later fitted with no fewer than five burners. A year later the lamp and its hot drinks were so popular that the crowds obstructing the square became an embarrassment and the vestry of St. Martin-in-the-Fields gave the owners of the infernal machine three months' notice to quit. The lamp was removed and gradually the others also disappeared.

The invention of the phonograph in America gave vending-machine designers further scope for ingenuity and for the first time, in 1890, a vending machine was given a voice. This was a weighing machine which not only registered the customer's weight but also played him an operatic aria as well. The idea was not a great success, but 'speak-your-weight' machines and fortune-telling machines and many other machines which use a sound mechanism have appeared from time to time ever since.

One of the most interesting contributions France made to the vending industry was the 'automatic fountain' which was installed in 1891 at a fair called, rather forbiddingly, the Exposition of Labour at the Palace of Industry. A reporter for the *Scientific American* wrote: 'In the automatic distributors of which we speak, it suffices to put a coin, say a five-cent piece, in a slot, when a tube placed beneath the money box allows a small glass of Malaga, a large glass of beer, etc., to flow. The apparatus operates with perfect regularity and the quantity of liquid is always accurately measured, its volume varying with its nature. There are distributors of this kind that serve hot liquids (such as coffee) or iced ones.'

At last the vending machine seemed to be moving into the sphere in which it was finally to make its fortune. The American reporter explained its merits to his readers. 'To the consumer, the automatic distribution offers the advantages of immediate delivering for a modest sum, and without any loss of time, an accurately measured quantity of hot or cold beverage furnished directly by the producer. The latter, selling his merchandise directly, can deliver it at a very low but remunerative price, and, through the aid of the apparatus with placards, circulars, etc., put at the consumer's disposal, can obtain the best of advertisements.' He could indeed, and these are the advantages which vending machines still have today.

The American reporter foresaw that the machines would be widely used, though not, it seems, necessarily by people like himself! '. . . In railway stations, public gardens, etc., it will be possible to utilize these apparatus . . . with the charitable object in view of furnishing the poor with wholesome and strengthening beverages (such as milk, bouillon, etc.) at a low price. . . .'

France also saw the appearance in 1893 of machines which dispensed a spray of scent, a device which became popular again in the 1940's and 1950's, and similar machines even supplied disinfectants and antiseptics in the same way. The public, in fact, seemed to like these machines as much as the perfume machines. By 1895 Germany had an automatic restaurant and in Belgium book vending was well established, but to a town in Utah, U.S.A., goes the final accolade for the most extraordinary use for a vending machine. For the price of two and a half dollars anyone wanting a divorce could get from a machine perfectly legal divorce papers which could be taken to the firm of solicitors whose name was printed on them and then filled in and witnessed.

At the turn of the century the vending machine was nearly fifty years old and still had not discovered its rightful place in society, and while it was still confined mostly to issuing chewing gum and stamped postcards, a thriving industry in gaming machines developed which for many years threatened to make the whole field of coin-operated machines rather questionable in the minds of many people. Then in 1902 vending took a major step forward with the opening in Philadelphia of the first American Automat. There had been automatic restaurants in Europe for nearly ten years, but the publicity which greeted the first American version proved to be the breakthrough which was to take the vending machine into organized catering.

The first major difficulty in the way of dispensing drinks from a machine was overcome in 1908 when the Public Cup Vendor Company of New York, later the Dixie Cup Company, introduced a vending machine which sold water in an individual paper cup. Soda pop had been sold for years from machines, but the customer had to take a cup from a row in front of the machine and rinse it in a tank of water before using it. Public Health officials did not care much for this system and the advent of the paper cup seemed to open the way for an enormous increase in the sale of drinks from machines. Surprisingly, it was twenty-five years before anyone put the idea into practice. Not until 1934 did a designer called Leslie Arnett manufacture and install as an experiment in Chicago's Lincoln Park Zoo the first self-contained, cup-type, soft-drink vending machine.

The soft-drink manufacturers immediately took up the idea. Coca-Cola sold bottled drinks from their refrigerated machines, and at last the vending industry began to get into its stride. The Vendo Company of Kansas was formed by an ex-real-estate man, Elmer F. Pierson, and three associates in 1936 and has grown into the biggest producer of vending machinery in the world. Vendo was joined by Vendrink, Masterdrink, Frostidrink, Coldrink and others, many of them small companies which merged after a few years.

From 1939 onwards Europe was engaged in a world war, and as a result the history of vending at this stage is exclusively American, but even in 1942 the vending industry still consisted for the most part of machines to sell sweets, cigarettes and soft drinks. In 1942 the production of vending machines practically ceased as all production capacity was required for the war effort and the machine manufacturers turned to making munitions for the American forces. Then, as the war effort intensified, industry made an interesting discovery: people could work harder and longer if they had a constant supply of hot drinks to keep them going. Management, who had believed that vending machines in factories would encourage the workers to waste time gossiping over cups of coffee, suddenly demanded vending machines by the thousand, and the manufacturers were forced to abandon their own war effort to go back to making vending machines in vain attempts to keep pace with the demand. At last the penny had dropped!

With the demand came many improvements. After the war a machine was developed which served coffee automatically in a cup. Before, a cup machine and a separate coffee machine had been necessary. In Philadelphia two ex-servicemen, Lloyd Rudd and K. C. Melikian, invented a hot-coffee vending machine, and although the vending industry refused to take their invention seriously at first, the public welcomed it and hot-coffee vending had made a start.

Why had it taken so long? In the first place a vending machine which dispenses hot coffee or tea and is in constant use usually needs plumbing, since a hand-filled water tank is too cumbersome. The machine also needs power to heat the water and this brings in safety factors. Lastly, there were flavour difficulties in the brewing of coffee and tea which had to be overcome by the tea and coffee companies before the machine manufacturers could dispense a satisfactory drink to the public. Then in the early 1950's Leslie Arnett, who had put the first cup-drink machine in Lincoln Park Zoo, unveiled the first coffee-vending machine that used ground coffee instead of liquid concentrate or instant dry ingredients.

In Britain the post-war vending boom came later and was slower than in the United States. There was a general shortage of money, and repairing the damage caused by the war took first priority. Also any significant extension of vending in the United Kingdom depended on the provision of an acceptable cup of tea, and this had to await the end of tea rationing. Britain had a greater tradition of personal service; the rich had always lived in a world of domestic servants, and even the less well off in their offices or workshops could expect their cups of tea and coffee to be brought to them on a tray or trolley. Americans were not so accustomed to being waited on and accepted more readily the principle of automation.

But the main reason was probably the different way that we in Britain manage our industrial catering. Here the practice has been for canteen meals and refreshments to be provided at cost price or less, and industrial firms have usually undertaken their own catering. Cheap and subsidized meals have become a 'fringe benefit' both accepted and expected in industry. In the United States industrial workers have always been accustomed to paying an economic price, and in that country industrial catering is usually put out to

I

contract to a specialist catering firm, which, of course, must make a profit to remain in business. So in America there was far greater incentive to take full advantage of vending as it developed.

On this side of the Atlantic, too, the first hot-drink machines developed from the cold-drink machines. In 1957 experiments were carried out with models that sold chilled milk. Many years ago some dairies had Iron Cows which dispensed a pennyworth of milk and there was one in the Willesden district of London as late as 1929. The new machine had the blessing of the Milk Marketing Board, and a pilot machine installed at Paddington Station sold 1,754 half-pint cartons of milk during Christmas week of 1957. Meanwhile, Joseph Sankey and Sons Ltd., manufacturing the American-designed Vendo machine under licence, found that in an average week about 1,000 cartons of milk were sold from a machine installed in a café in central London, even though milk by the glass could also be bought over the counter.

Milk machines raised fresh problems not experienced with earlier kinds of vending, problems which gave a foretaste of what was going to happen before the vastly more complicated business of tea- and coffee-vending was successfully accomplished. The machine contained a refrigeration unit to maintain the milk at the correct temperature of 42°F. It had to be sterilized regularly and a rigorous programme of cleaning and maintenance was required. Nevertheless, milk machines were a reasonably successful proposition from the late 1950's onwards and became even more so when they were developed to sell milk drinks of various flavours. From then on it could only be a matter of time before engineers' minds were turned to the question of vending Britain's two most popular drinks, tea and coffee. There were three ways of tackling the problem of ingredients. Liquid concentrates could be used, prepared beforehand, or instant ingredients in dry, powder form, or fresh leaf tea and ground coffee. All had their advantages and disadvantages.

Among the first manufacturers in the field were W. M. Still and Sons Ltd. Encouraged by the growing number of milk machines in use, they decided on the liquid concentrate, using a similar kind of refrigeration to chill the concentrated tea or coffee so that it would keep in good condition and retain its flavour. There were two separate machines, called the Tea Cub and the Coffee Cub, and they were complicated affairs because they had to include boilers (to heat the water) as well as chilling units.

The Tea Cub was advertised as 'Britain's first fully automatic tea machine'. It used fresh milk and a switch was fitted for customers to choose whether they wanted tea with or without sugar. The capacity was 250 6 oz. cups, and the cost was claimed to be less than 1d. (½p) per cup.

'Industry', said Still's advertising literature, 'has gone to great expense in providing staff amenities, yet has largely ignored what, to a nation of tea-drinkers, should have been the most obvious—the provision of a warming cup of tea on arrival. Staff members frequently face long demoralizing periods of travel to reach their place of work. What can more surely set them up to start the day right than a freshly made cup of tea?'

Still's had got hold of a very telling point. In many offices the coffee is brought round almost as soon as the staff have arrived and got settled in because it has been found that until they get their coffee many people can hardly get on with their work at all. Vending machines would supply a need in factories which had hardly been realized before. Both the Tea Cub and its predecessor, the Coffee Cub (which was launched in 1956), were American machines from Rudd-Melikian Inc., the pioneers of hot-coffee vending, and they were made under licence in this country. More than ten years later a number of these machines are still in use and giving satisfactory service.

In 1958 National Automatic Machines Ltd. introduced their Perky machine which was among the first to use leaf tea. This too was a complex piece of apparatus, its operation being based on forty individual canisters in which tea was brewed. These were positioned round a revolving drum, each canister holding sixteen cups of tea. As each canister was emptied, the next one rolled into the dispensing position and was filled with hot water. When the complete sequence of forty canisters had been used the machine had to be opened up and each canister recharged with leaf tea, and the process was then repeated. But like the liquid concentrate machine, this type too had a refrigerating unit, as fresh milk was used and this had to be maintained at the correct temperature.

Normally a factory will either buy its vending machines and ingredients and operate them itself or rent the vending machines from an operating company who will be responsible for maintenance and supplying the ingredients. In either case it is essential that someone has some knowledge of the ingredients which go into the machines, and in practice there is quite a lot to know. Leaf tea, as opposed to spray or accelerated freeze-dried tea, presents the greatest difficulty because of the time taken to infuse. Vending machines usually have a seven-second cycle which does not give the tea leaves enough time to infuse properly, resulting in a weak brew. It is often necessary to experiment to find a suitable blend of small-leafed, quick-brew teas which will react satisfactorily in the small time allowed.

Some manufacturers, however, have now assisted further by designing a mechanism which extracts more flavour from the tea in the time it takes for the cycle to be completed.

When vending machines first began to make their mark in British industrial catering early in the 1960's most of the machines produced in Britain were American machines made here under licence. This had the advantage that the users of the machines could enjoy the benefit of America's experience, and soon the British manufacturers began to develop their own ideas. But for a long time their designers were restricted by the price that the customer was prepared to pay for the machines. Also the ingredients available in the early years did not do justice to the machines' capabilities and it was not until the ingredient manufacturers improved the quality of their products that their great potential was fully admitted. Workers, on their part, displayed an almost perverse preference for the tea-trolley tea, however bad, rather than vending-machine tea, however good. Only when the tea trolleys were firmly banished for good did the majority of people accept them as a reasonable and even superior substitute.

Gloster, Ditchburn and Sankey were some of the names which came to dominate the market in hot-drink machines. Sankey, which was associated with the Vendo Company of the United States, received a great boost when the company became part of the big Guest, Keen and Nettlefold group. Gloster, of course, were originally a famous aircraft company and at first vending machines played only a small part in their diversification programme, but by 1959 they had developed a wall-mounted tea and coffee machine, another new innovation. Like Still's, this type used liquid concentrates as did a larger version which followed.

A big campaign was started by people concerned with productivity and efficency, politicians among them, to combat the wasteful extravagance of conventional tea and coffee service in factories. It was found that industrial workers were having to walk long distances to get their tea, and then had to stand in queues. Often it took longer to get the drink than to drink it. Where a tea-trolley service was provided, the cost was found to be staggering. In one small establishment with a staff of forty a part-time 'tea lady' was employed to make the morning coffee and afternoon tea, take it round to the workers and wash up afterwards. When the whole operation was costed the figures showed that the tea and coffee were costing the company 1s. 10d. (9p) per cup! The figures on a nation-wide estimate were even more dramatic. A £20-a-week employee wasted 2d. (1p) for each lost minute of his working shift. Added to this was the cost of lost machine time, factory and staff overheads. The lost minutes added up to a fantastic sum each year for tea breaks, when expensive automation processes, costly production machinery and highly paid labour all came to a halt. Meanwhile canteen costs were rising rapidly and managements had to consider some alternative. People doing research on the subject of industrial fatigue discovered that the tea breaks did not, in any case, always have the expected galvanizing effect on all the workers. Experiments in which the blood-sugar level of workers was measured under actual working conditions showed that when breaks were allowed when mental fatigue began, efficiency improved. Food and drink were more valuable than just rest and workers who needed to concentrate more needed more breaks. If food and drinks were always available, not only did efficiency improve, but so did the general health of the workers, with all the benefits, such as reduced absenteeism and a happier working atmosphere, which followed. Such a service could only be provided by vending machines which would dispense not only drinks of various sorts but also sandwiches and hot food as well. Some years ago in America someone invented a hot-dog machine which delivered into the customer's hands a dog so hot that he could not hold it. The machine did not survive long, but the idea did, and it has proved particularly valuable to night-shift workers, and also to workers on the early shift who miss their breakfast at home but are awake enough to start being hungry by the time they reach work.

Vending machines have increased substantially in price over the years. Some of the early ones which sold at less than £300 were really underpriced and as a result some manufacturers found themselves in difficulty for lack of development capital. Today's large vending machine for industrial use may cost more, but much of the increase is due to the fact that the modern machine is a far more sophisticated piece of equipment. One of its sophistications resulted from the need to defeat the misguided enthusiasm of the mischievous and sometimes downright dishonest public. People who would not try to cheat a shopkeeper or café proprietor seemed to regard 'beating the machine' as a personal challenge. This was not a new problem for vending-machine manufacturers, but with the development of hot-drink and other machines in the 1950's and 1960's the ingenuity of the tricksters knew no bounds. Students in a technical college were even found to be using discs of frozen carbon dioxide (which subsequently evaporated) to cheat their drinks machine. It was the operators who first felt the effect if any fraudulent practice was going on, and operating companies became necessary from the first.

In the early days the operators led an eventful life. In one case, where a machine was obviously not taking as much money as it should, someone discovered that by taking three-quarters of a cup of tea from the machine, and then at the vital moment throwing the switch to 'coffee', one could get a cup of coffee without paying any more money. The manufacturers refused to believe that this was possible until they had a personal demonstration; they then had to devise a completely new set of electrical relays for their machine. Apart from fraud, the operators had to contend with misuse. The machines too had their teething troubles. Some workers liked to pour coffee dregs into the coin mechanism. The luckless operators were called out at all hours to put things right. Some of the misuse was sheer vandalism, for factory workers did not always take vending machines to their hearts. In some cases, where they had had their own private arrangements for tea breaks, they strongly objected to being obliged to use the machine instead and pay for their tea.

It was small wonder that some of the early operators despaired and found other, easier, ways of earning a living, but the hardy ones persevered and established what have now become very prosperous businesses. The operating companies in fact perform a very valuable job of communication between the machine manufacturers, the users of the machines and the ingredient suppliers who need to be kept informed of the machine's demands and performance and the reactions of the customers. There was at first a considerable built-in prejudice against vended drinks, especially tea. Instant coffee and chocolate were accepted first, but it took a long time before the average British customer could be persuaded that a drinkable cup of tea could be obtained from a machine instead of a teapot. Gradually, with improvements in the machines and in the type of tea used in them, the customer was won round. Manufacturers have also developed all sorts of devices to make their machines foolproof and knave-proof, so that wilful sabotage is now much less frequent.

Vending has become an accepted part of modern life and is sure to play an even larger role in the future. Yet very few people understand how a modern vending machine works and so they are unreasonably suspicious about the quality and freshness of the drinks which are dispensed from them. Four essentials are required for the vending operation: water supply, electricity, ingredients and cups.

The large-capacity machine must be plumbed into the water supply. No special electrical installation is required. A vending machine can be plugged into an ordinary 13 or 15 amp wall socket. Water is supplied to a tank which contains an electric heating element, thermostatically controlled to maintain the water at a temperature between 65° and 75°C. This is the most suitable temperature for vending because the beverage is not then too hot for immediate drinking. For this reason vending ingredients are produced to dissolve instantly in this temperature range. Machines which also sell cold drinks are fitted with a second water tank in which a refrigeration unit keeps the temperature down to around 7°C.

The ingredients are placed in separate containers which rest side by side. A typical range would include tea, coffee, milk powder, sugar, drinking chocolate and soup. The cups are usually of 7 oz. capacity and are made to stack in columns or turrets which are stored inside the machine. In some cases the mechanism can be adjusted to accommodate either tall or squat-shaped cups.

The customer inserts his coin of the value required, and modern machines will sell drinks at up to four different prices. First the mechanism tests the coin not only for size, weight and thickness, but also for metal content, milling and even the absence of a hole in the middle. Having defeated the most common type of fraud, the machine accepts the coin, at the same time closing a relay to permit a sale of the appropriate value.

The customer presses the selection button which in turn closes the necessary switches to set the operation in motion. The water valve functions first, releasing the appropriate volume of water into the mixing trough, then an electric motor turns an auger screw fitted in the bottom of each of the canisters of ingredient. The powder is forced out of the container on the same principle as a mincing machine. The motor runs for precisely the time required to dispense the right quantity of ingredients. Each ingredient descends into the running water and the mixture flows into the waiting cup.

The length of time that it takes to obtain a drink is in most machines only eight seconds from the insertion of the coin, though leaf-tea machines may take rather longer. The working of the auger screw must be accurately timed so that it is completed before the cupful of water has stopped passing down the trough, allowing the water to take away every trace of the powdered ingredient to avoid tainting the next vend. At the same time the delivery pipe is kept continually clean and rinsed.

Another method of dispensing ingredients is to fit two wheels horizontally in the base of the containers. The lower wheel has one hole through it and the upper one has four holes. Only the upper wheel is connected to the motor. When the motor is operated the upper wheel turns, carrying a quantity of ingredient in each of its holes. When one of these coincides with the single hole in the wheel beneath the measured amount of ingredient falls into the mixing trough or bowl.

Although in the majority of machines the customer has to insert his coin first, there are others which work on the pre-selection principle. In these machines the customers must set the machine to the required drink and then put in the coin, which itself sets the machine in operation.

While all these developments were going on with the large vending machines, the first dispensing machines were appearing on the market. These machines usually consisted of a row of containers rather like milk bottles upside down holding powdered ingredients held in a rack arrangement. At the base of each dispenser was a mechanism which deposited an appropriate amount of ingredient into a cup. Hot water came from a flash-type boiler usually filled from a storage tank holding as much as three gallons. The machines varied in size but were either fixed to a wall or stood on a table which led them to have the general description of table-top dispensing machines.

The modern machines available today, sturdy and reliable, are a great improvement on some of the earlier models. In the days before all the machines had been improved I learned to my cost that it was the agent and distributor like myself who bore the brunt of the test marketing and service problems. Taps jammed or blew off, tanks leaked or blew up, drip-trays overflowed or fell off and the electric circuitry was positively dangerous, as securing brackets for the solenoids shook loose and the circuit fused.

The important thing for customers to know about vending machines is that every drink they get from them is fresh. The old lady on Paddington Station was worrying unnecessarily when she refused to have a cup of tea from a vending machine because 'you never know how long it has been made'. There is no large tank which is filled with hot tea first thing in the morning to be drawn off a cupful at a time during the rest of the day!

Manufacturers of both dispensing machines and the more complicated vending machines are always looking for ways to reduce maintenance costs and cut out as many points of breakdown as possible. One improvement will be solid state electrical circuitry which will enable the existing circuit board to be unclipped and a new one installed without putting the machine out of use. Electric impulsing will eventually replace customer-controlled operations like pressing buttons and pulling out drawers. The measuring mechanism controlling the supply of ingredients will become even

Left, Old stamp vending machine made in 1892.

Right, A 'chicken machine' which sold metal eggs for 1d. Each egg contained a trinket and the hen clucked as it was delivered. In use in 1908.

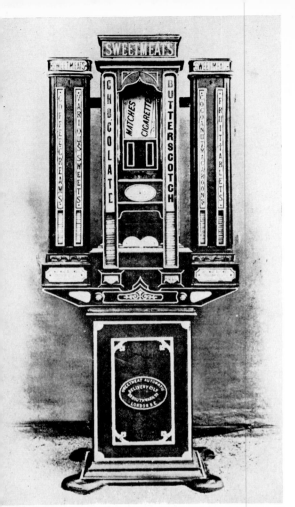

A typical machine which dispensed sweets and cigarettes, once familiar on every railway platform.

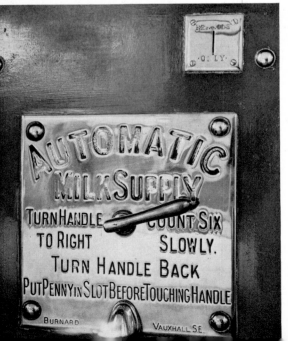

A fifty-year-old milk vending machine which dispensed milk by the pennyworth.

In 1898 this streetlamp was erected in Leicester Square. It dispensed cocoa or hot coffee and concentrated tablets of beef tea which could then be dissolved in boiling water. The water was heated in the tank at the top and was dispensed for ½d. per quart. It attracted vast crowds and was removed within a year because it was thought to be a public nuisance.

We like to preserve a few of the firm's relics from the past.

Modern vending machines. *Above*, on the shop floor; *below*, in an office canteen. Microwave ovens have been incorporated into this bank of vending machines which heat the meals in seconds.

The interior of a modern hot and cold drinks vending machine.

A table-top dispensing machine which contains a selection of concentrated drinks which the operator dissolves in hot water dispensed from the machine.

'A comfortable dish of tea in high life' from an engraving published in 1782.

Tea caddy with two compartments and blending bowl made by Asprey of Bond Street with a Bramah lock. Early nineteenth century.

Anna, Duchess of Bedford, who transformed tea-time by adding cakes and turning it into a light meal.

more accurate and reliable and drip-proof and dust-proof components will eliminate the cause of most machine failures.

The vending industry as we think of it today is still an astonishingly young industry, yet already it is a vital part of every factory's plans to increase productivity and efficiency. Its allies are its rapidly rising sales and its increasing acceptance by the general public. There are many refinements and developments to vending machines which can only come as the economic outlook of the industry becomes more secure, but when that happens, and we can confidently expect perfect service at the drop of a coin, we shall wonder how we ever did without them.

10

The Social Life of Tea

It is so obvious as to be hardly worth mentioning that at the present time coffee enjoys a higher social status than tea. This is partly because of the strange and expensive image that coffee still enjoys, even though it becomes more popular every day and because, even without the competition from coffee, tea has come down in the world.

One of the reasons for this is that tea, in the packet, is cheap, and while other groceries have risen in price tea prices have remained virtually unchanged for a decade until 1970. Since any advertising theorists with a bent for psychology will tell us that people always value what they have to pay a lot for, this stability alone would seem to have been harmful, but there have also been other causes at work.

Undoubtedly one of the most important factors is the association that tea has come to have with national crises and grim endurance of the less interesting kind. As time becomes more valuable and housewives dispense with the afternoon ritual with a silver tray and delicate china cups, so the field is left to the homely brown pot and the general atmosphere of pulling ourselves together. This is a great pity, for not only does it mean that people tend to be less willing to give their attention and discrimination to buying and making good tea, but the products of hundreds of years of the silversmith's and china-maker's art are left in the cupboard or on the shelves of museums.

It is also unfortunate that journalists and headline writers so frequently succumb to the temptation to write about tea in terms of 'cuppas', 'cups that cheer' and 'one for the pot'. The prestige of tea would benefit enormously if only these dreadful expressions would go out of fashion.

A visit to any archaeological museum leaves little doubt that the basis of civilization is the pot, in all its various forms. Notwithstanding all the modern techniques, carbon dating and the rest, that have come to archaeology in recent years, pottery is still the principal means of identifying and dating the cultures of the past, and who can doubt that archaeologists of the future will describe the teapot and coffee-pot as the characteristic artifacts of the last couple of centuries?

Wherever Englishmen went and colonized, from British Guiana to British North Borneo, the teapot has gone with them and the British expansion of the Victorian era coincided with the advance of tea. In contrast, however, the coffee pot has never achieved quite the same affection, nor does it seem to have attracted so much attention from the craftsman. Coffee missed the great days of workmanship and now that it is really coming into its own, it is the manufacturers of more sophisticated coffee machines who will reap the benefit.

In ancient China, tea was brewed in unglazed stoneware pots, usually red or brown in colour. Some were sternly utilitarian articles while others were elaborately decorated. The Chinese believed that pots made from this material gave a better flavour to the tea than any made of procelain. Chinese teapots were sent over to Europe with some of the early consignments of tea, and the Dutch potters soon imitated them. The earliest English silver teapot, which had a strange near-conical shape, dates from 1670. Later a Dutch craftsman settled in Staffordshire and when he made his first English stoneware teapot in 1693 a whole industry was born, but it was not until the eighteenth century that the Germans specialized in superb porcelain teapots.

Because it is a utensil which is to be put to a practical use, the design of the teapot has fairly severe limitations. It has to be large enough to hold a reasonable number of cups of tea, yet not too heavy to lift when full. It has to be easy to handle when full of nearly boiling water, easy to clean, well balanced at different angles and not easily knocked over. Since these requirements mean that the basic shape is virtually unalterable, the designers from the beginning concentrated on decoration and a variety of materials for making the pots. These ranged from heavy and precious metals to delicate and costly porcelain so fragile and exquisitely hand-painted that only a wealthy and confident generation could have regarded them as practical at all. These teapots were, of course, mostly intended for the rich. The more workaday versions of the latter half of the eighteenth and of the nineteenth centuries would in most cases not seem out of place in a modern kitchen. For a time, in the eighteenth century, there appeared as an ancillary to the teapot industry a whole succession of hot-milk jugs, many of silver in a variety of shapes and sizes. There were pear-shaped jugs, six-sided jugs and eight-sided ones. They enjoyed a brief vogue before it was realized that hot milk was not really necessary at all and that cold milk or cream would do just as well.

Teapots, in their present-day, more utilitarian, form, are likely to be with us for a long time yet, but there are signs that eventually we may switch perhaps to filter machines which will make both tea and coffee and eliminate the teapot altogether.

Although tea has what is known in the publicity world as a 'feminine image', this was not always so. During the eighteenth century the public pleasure gardens of London, which had originally been tea-less and not too respectable, changed their character and turned themselves into tea gardens. They had a season from April or May to early autumn and although all sorts of drinks were available, including coffee and chocolate, tea acquired an outstanding vogue. Vauxhall, Marylebone and Cuper's gardens had a fixed admission charge of a shilling and refreshments were extra, but at Ranelagh, perhaps the most famous pleasure gardens of all, tea, coffee and bread and butter were included in the admission charge of half a crown (13p), which was a lot of money in 1742 when the gardens were opened.

Vauxhall Gardens had the longest and most successful history. It was a short distance east of Vauxhall Bridge and was opened in 1732 on the site of the New Spring Gardens which had acquired a dubious reputation. Vauxhall Gardens had lantern-lit walks and music, suppers and fireworks. The fashionable came in great numbers and so did many other people who liked to mingle with the rich. The famous bandstand and pipe organ seem a very tame form of entertainment today, but in their time they kept Vauxhall Gardens in the forefront of popular places to go during most of the eighteenth and half of the nineteenth centuries. Vauxhall Gardens was at its zenith in the years from 1750 to 1790 when Horace Walpole, Henry Fielding and Dr. Johnson used to go there with their literary friends.

Ranelagh Gardens was up in Chelsea, and as soon as it opened in 1742 it became a serious rival to Vauxhall. The garden was developed from the grounds of the Earl of Ranelagh's house which had been bought by the owner of the Drury Lane Theatre after the Earl had died, and it was run as a limited company. Ranelagh was not nearly so big or so rural as Vauxhall, but it had a small canal or lake with a Chinese house and a Venetian temple in the middle of it.

The greatest attraction apart from the exclusiveness of the patrons, was the great Rotunda. Inside it was a circular room 150 feet in diameter with a double tier of boxes around the entire wall. There was a highly ornate colonnade to support the roof and a huge fireplace in case the evenings were cool. This meant that the gardens could be used for a much greater part of the year for concerts and masquerades. It was so orderly and still that Samuel Rogers, the poet, wrote that 'you could hear the whishing sound of the ladies' trains as the immense assembly walked round and round the room'.

Walking round the Rotunda was in fact the chief amusement of the place and those tired of walking would retire to one of the boxes around the walls to be served with tea and bread and butter which would strengthen them for more exercise.

Another famous tea gardens on the outskirts of London was Marylebone. It was owned by Daniel Gough, who laid it out on the site of a former tavern and bowling green. There was room for supper parties and balls, and orchestras and the inevitable pipe organ supplied music for concerts and dancing. Horace Walpole, who was a great frequenter of tea gardens, has written of the statue-lined walks and fireworks at Marylebone, but there were occasional fights and there are also records of scandalous behaviour by the Duke of Cumberland. Marylebone attracted its greatest number of notables, including Handel, in the late 1750's when some excellent music used to be performed. Pergolesi's exquisite little comic opera *La Serva Padrona* had its première there, but after a time its fortunes changed with its ownership and in 1776 it closed for ever.

Cuper's Gardens, just south of Waterloo Bridge, had great attractions for those who liked a trip on the river. It had a landing stage on the Thames and a short lane led to the entrance. Again there was music, and, of course, there was tea. It was run by Mrs. Evans, widow of the first owner, and so long as she kept tight control of the running of it, Cuper's Gardens was a fashionable and select success. However, rowdyism eventually crept in, and Cuper's came to an end with a final concert in 1759.

Tea *al fresco* was therefore firmly established, at least in the lives of Londoners, as early as the middle of the eighteenth century. Afternoon tea in the drawing room came a few years later, and for this custom we must thank Anna, the wife of the seventh Duke of Bedford. In her day it was customary to eat a huge breakfast, lunch was of little account and dinner was at eight o'clock or thereabouts. It was not surprising that round about five o'clock in the afternoon the Duchess used to get what she described as 'a sinking feeling'. She therefore ordered tea and cakes to be served in the afternoon and the fashion spread among those of her acquaintance who had noticed the same uncomfortable symptoms. Fanny Kemble, the actress, first encountered afternoon tea at Belvoir Castle while she was visiting the Duke and Duchess of Rutland and believed that afternoon tea as an established meal probably originated around that time; it was essentially a female ritual and it remained fashionable until very recently.

Once women became accustomed to tea and cakes in the afternoon at home, they began to expect them to be provided in cafés too.
By the early years of this century the demand for afternoon tea 'out'
reached its peak and all hotels and department stores served it,
and it became a very important part of every kind of social event.
Ascot, Wimbledon, Henley and the royal garden parties would not
be the same without the essential and soothingly familiar ritual of
the cup of tea and cake, which not only refreshes the revellers but
provides a recognizable routine which holds such functions together
quite as much as the programme of events. As in the days of the
pleasure gardens, tea and music became associated once more. The
tinkling of the teacups was accompanied by the tinkling of a piano
and the scraping of a violinist and cellist playing selections from
Franz Lehar operettas and morsels arranged by Kreisler.

The first real tea shop was opened in 1717 by Thomas Twining
who had taken over *Tom's Coffee House* and renamed it *The Golden
Lion*. Once tea establishments had started on their own independent
existence—independent, that is, from coffee houses—they attracted
a following of their own. By the early 1900's it was very much the
thing for the upper classes in London to go to *Gunter's* or *Rumpelmeyer's* for afternoon tea. These very exclusive tea shops were pri-
marily confectioners, *Gunter's*, for instance, was famous for its ices,
but tea was served in the same way that *Demel's* and *Gerstner's* in
Vienna served coffee as well as the most exquisite cakes in Europe.
There was a *Rumpelmeyer's* in New York and ex-patriate English
and Americans in Paris went to *Rumpelmeyer's* in the Rue de Rivoli,
but true English tea as a meal was founded in 1900 in the Place de
la Concorde when the Brothers Neal, who were stationers, began to
serve tea and biscuits on two tables at the end of the counter. *Neal's*
became the renowned *W. H. Smith & Son's Tea Rooms*, as much a
haven to Englishwomen as the American pharmacy was to Americans. The first modern tea room in Paris was the *Kardomah* and soon
there were many places where French people as well as foreigners
could stave off that 'sinking feeling'.

Hotels served tea too, and since hotels also often had orchestras,
a social custom arose which seems rather strange now and is
entirely extinct. This was the *thé dansant*. Around five o'clock in the
afternoon young men, presumably with no pressing need to earn
a living, were to be seen at hotels like the Ritz fox-trotting with
débutantes in hats and coats. *Thé dansants* survived right through the
years between the wars, but the 1939 war finally killed them off.

Further down the social scale came the tea shops as we still know
them, the places where the majority of people went for a good cup

of tea without a lot of jigging about. There were already many places in Kensington and Mayfair which had a few tables where suburban ladies could take tea after an afternoon's shopping, but the pioneers in tea rooms for the general public were the Aerated Bread Company or A.B.C.

The elderly manageress of the company's bread and cake shop near London Bridge Station made a practice of sharing her pot of tea with one or two favoured customers in her back room. This proved so popular that she suggested to the company that serving tea should become a regular part of its trade. The directors agreed, and the London Bridge tea shop became the first of many.

That was in 1884. A few years later Montague Gluckstein, then a travelling partner in a tobacco business, found it difficult to obtain any refreshments on his journeys except in licensed houses. His business acumen realized the opportunity. He suggested to a group of his relatives that they should form a company and go into non-alcoholic catering. One of them, who became chairman, gave his name to the business; he was Joseph Lyons. In 1894 the first Lyons tea shop was opened at 48 Piccadilly, London. The Lyons policy of quick service and good value for money proved instantly successful, and now there are few towns of any size without a Lyons tea shop. Subsequently Lyons went into the wholesale food trade and have many diverse subsidiary companies, but the two products for which they are still best known are tea and cakes.

There were also any number of smaller companies and private individuals who opened tea rooms and cafes, often with much charm and imagination, to appeal to shoppers and tourists wherever they might need something to revive them in the morning or after-noon.

Every year Britain imports about 500 million pounds of tea. The rest of Europe, excluding Russia, imports about 116 million pounds. European countries, are in the main, coffee consumers, although this does not mean that the coffee that they import is necessarily any better in quality than the coffee imported into this country. The idea that the quality of coffee drunk abroad is better than ours is mistaken. Also, many European countries have a considerable wine industry which provides them with a further reasonably cheap alternative to tea. The greatest consumption of tea per head in con-tinental Europe is in Holland, which has similar historical connec-tions as Great Britain with the tea-producing countries. The Dutch have been drinking tea even longer than we have. They prepare it in exactly the same way and have much the same tastes in tea, except that, naturally, more of their tea comes from Indonesia.

In other European countries tea-drinking is unusual, except among tourists. Even the equipment for making it hardly exists. Englishwomen hoping to avoid the continental tea bag by taking packets of their own favourite tea often discover to their amazement that there are rarely any teapots and often no kettles. The tea bag is put directly into the cup because that is the only method of making the tea, and while there is no contradicting the very English name which is printed on the label attached to the little string, it is always noticeable that the tea, for whatever reason, does not taste the same as a pot of tea made at home from the packet with the same name.

The greatest consumer of tea in Europe as a whole must be Russia. Although no exact figures are available, the population of Russia is more than 200 million so the annual consumption of tea must be enormous. For many years Russia imported tea from China and until recently a good deal of China tea (together with tea from other producing countries) was still sold to Russia for reasons of trade and balance of payments between the two countries, as well as for traditional reasons. Nevertheless, Russia is a tea-producing country herself and has considerable tea estates in Georgia. The 'Russian tea' spoken of in this country does not, of course, mean tea from Georgia, only that it is drunk without milk and is served in a glass.

The Russians have been tea-drinkers for more than three centuries and have customs all of their own. One of the most important is that by tradition they have one enormous meal a day which combines lunch and dinner and is eaten around our afternoon-tea time. Throughout the rest of the day they make do with constant cups of tea, and this is why they need the samovar, which provides everlasting supplies of boiling water. To English people the Russian samovar is an incomprehensible method of making tea by means of a machine. In fact the samovar is only a water boiler and does not make the tea at all. Basically there is an urn of water with a tube going up the middle which contains red-hot charcoal. When the water boils it can be drawn off by means of a tap into an ordinary English-type teapot with tea leaves in it. The teapot is then put to stand on top of the samovar to keep warm while the tea brews. The tea is made very strong so that when it is poured out the glass is only partly filled and then topped up with more boiling water from the samovar. The tea is drunk with lemon, since milk and cream have always been rarities in Russia.

Russians take their tea with sugar but instead of putting the lumps of sugar in the tea, the Russian peasants put them in their

The start of the five-o'clock-tea idea in England, from a contemporary print.

The poet John Gay and his sisters, *circa* 1720.
    'At noon, (the lady's matin hour)
     I sip the tea's delicious flower.'

Thé à l'Anglaise at the Court of the Prince de Conti in the eighteenth century. A painting by Michael Barthélemy in the Musée du Louvre, Paris. The pianist is the young Mozart.

The Rotunda in Ranelagh Gardens with the Company at Breakfast, 1751.

Worcester teapot decorated by Fidele Duvivier, 1772.

A Chinese teapot with the inscription: 'The water of the stream of
Chu has a delight equal to the sight of the mountain gorges.' The
waters of Chu were much esteemed for making tea. This teapot
bears the mark *Yi Hsing Imperial Ware*.

Silver teapot, 1783–4. Made by Hester Bateman.

Silver teapot, 1706–7. Made by David Willaume, one of the Huguenot silversmiths working in England.

mouths and then drink the tea through the sugar. Another variation is to put a spoonful of jam in the tea in place of lemon.

The producing countries themselves consume a good deal of the tea they produce, although the tendency is for the best tea to be exported to world markets. Since China is by far the biggest tea-producing country and the Chinese are believed to be among the world's largest tea-drinkers *per capita*, the amount of tea consumed in that country must almost be beyond belief. In 1845 Robert Fortune in his book *Wanderings in China* estimated it at 1,800 million pounds and it must have trebled since then because of the increase in the population.

The China tea that the Chinese drink never was quite the China tea which we used to know in this country. Although the richer Chinese used to drink black tea of the kind exported to this country, it was not new tea, since they kept it in sealed earthen jars for a couple of years before using it to moderate the pungent quality which new tea always has. The oldest way of making tea, still followed at least until recent years in some parts of China, was to boil the powdered tea with rice cakes into a thick, syrupy substance. The bitter taste was removed by adding ginger.

In Japan, which is also a great tea-consuming country, green tea is the most widely used and it has an ancient and complicated etiquette which every girl of good family learns as part of her classical education. At least three years of instruction and practice are necessary to acquire complete mastery of the subtleties of the ceremony.

If Japan can claim the most elegant associations with tea, Tibet must surely have the most revolting to English tastes. Since very early times, boiled and churned butter-tea has been the great stand-by of the Tibetans. No Tibetan drinks less than fifteen cups a day, and some even seventy or eighty. The butter, which is made from goats' milk, is usually rancid.

The Mongols and Tartars make a kind of soup from powdered brick tea from China which they boil with alkaline steppe water, salt and fat. Then they strain it and mix it with milk, butter and roasted meal. In Korea they drop tea leaves from Japan into a kettle of boiling water and serve it with raw eggs and rice cakes. The eggs are sucked from the shells between sips of tea and the cakes are eaten when the eggs are finished. The Burmese pickle their tea or steep it in oil; the Siamese chew theirs with salt and other condiments. In Cashmere, tea is boiled in a tinned copper pot, and red potash, aniseed and a little salt are added; in Turkestan they like cream tea, which has no resemblance to a Devon tea. The tea is boiled in a

K

tinned copper pot until it is very strong. The cream, from goats' milk, is added while the tea is boiling and bits of bread are soaked in it.

There is practically nothing that cannot be done with tea, from staining the floor with it to stuffing the leaves into pillows, but these are just curiosities. Anyone wanting a good cup of tea merely has to pour freshly boiling water on to a reasonable quantity of good tea. How weak or how strong the tea should be is purely a matter of personal preference, and so is the kind of tea used. Different growing areas produce different characteristics in their tea; the tea trade knows its job, and the quality is fairly represented by the price charged.

*　　　*　　　*　　　*　　　*

Few products can claim as long an advertising history as tea. The earliest-known advertisement for it was, understandably, Chinese, and it was in the form of a book, the *Ch'a Ching*, mentioned in Chapter 7. Lu Yu, the world's first copy-writer, did such a good job that later on, when the Chinese merchants wanted to hide the secrets of tea-making, the 'foreign devils' were able to piece together enough information from the *Ch'a Ching* for them to imitate the Chinese.

The next advertisement was Japanese, *Kitcha Yojoki*, or the 'Book of Tea Sanitation', an unhappy title but apt, since the author, Yaisai, was mostly concerned with the medicinal properties of tea.

It was not until 1658 that the first advertisement for tea appeared in a newspaper, the *Mercurius Politicus* of London, and it said:

'That Excellent, and by all Physitians approved, *China* drink, called by the *Chineans, Tcha*, by other Nations Tay alias Tee, is sold at the *Sultanesshead*, a *Cophee-house* in *Sweetings* Rents by the Royal Exchange, *London*.'

This announcement followed an advertisement offering a reward for the apprehension of a horse thief.

Other coffee houses which also sold tea began to advertise the fact, and in 1680 tea dealers put notices in the newspapers to inform prospective customers of the kinds of tea they had available. This developed into brand advertising as we know it which continues into the television age.

At the same time that tea companies were advertising the qualities of their own teas, from the late nineteenth century onwards, the producing countries also found it worth their while to extol, in a general way, the qualities of the different growths. China, whose exports of tea were in rapid decline from the turn of the century, did not take part in this publicity campaign, but India and Ceylon, who were anxious to secure greater shares of an expanding market, if possible at China's expense, spent a good deal of money on tea propaganda. The campaigns were financed at first by voluntary contributions from the estate owners, but publicity on a large scale required more funds and a compulsory tea cess had to be levied on all who planted tea. The publicity campaign was world-wide, although special attention was given to the United States, which had a large population and was almost completely ignorant of Indian and Ceylon tea. In this country the appeal was mostly to people's loyalty to the empire, and some of the advertising was, to say the least, remarkable. There was, for instance, a full-page advertisement in *Ladies Home Journal* for October 1897 which showed Queen Victoria entertaining President Cleveland to tea. 'Mr. President,' Her Majesty is saying, 'may I offer you a cup of pure tea from Ceylon and India?' This is only one of many instances where Queen Victoria was recruited by commercial interests to help increase sales, and they must have given the general public many misconceptions about life at the Palace.

The China tea trade by the 1930's was dead, but it was still not lying down. In 1931 the sales of 'foreign' teas in London was troubling the Indian Tea Association and the Ceylon and South Indian Association so much that they launched a movement which became the 'Buy British' campaign of 1931–3 and led to the reimposition of the British preferential tea duty. The Empire Marketing Board, the Trade Commissioner for India, the Chief Commissioner for H.M. East African Dependencies and a majority of the important English tea-blending and -packing firms all joined in and about 1,500 municipal authorities adopted a rule of specifying Empire growths when they advertised for tenders of tea for public institutions. In 1935 the joint Empire tea propaganda campaign was being run by the Empire Tea Market-Expansion Board. In 1939, when war broke out, the Ministry of Food became the sole purchasers of tea for the United Kingdom requirements, the Mincing Lane auctions were suspended and the public drank what it could get. Not until tea rationing ended in 1952 did the tea-producing countries have another opportunity to promote their individual merits.

Today the Indian Tea Board and the Ceylon Tea Board carry on the work of promoting their countries' teas, and in some fields they also work together. The Ceylon Tea Board in particular has done a most admirable job of making the public aware of the merits of Ceylon tea, and its idea of putting on sale four teas typifying the four main tea-growing areas of Ceylon has been a deserved success. The first-class public relations carried on through the Ceylon Tea Centre is, of course, the outward manifestation of a very acute awareness by the Ceylon Government of the vital importance of its tea exports. In this Ceylon has been much more sophisticated than India, which has not been nearly so successful in marshalling her tea industry to help the national economy.

Probably the most interesting phenomenon in tea advertising in recent years has been the 'Join the Tea Set' campaign. Those interested in promoting the sales of tea in this country had been aware that coffee was gaining in popularity, particularly among the young. Anything so much favoured by older people was almost bound to be unpopular with the young. But there may have been other reasons too. More women started to go out to work, which meant that they were no longer at home in the afternoon drinking tea. Working hours for men tended to become shorter, so that they came home to an evening meal and tea with the family and the extra pot of afternoon tea was dispensed with. Children coming home from school for their tea drank less tea with it, mostly due to the increasing popularity of soft drinks and the publicity of the Milk Marketing Board on behalf of milk. Now that so many people are accustomed to an adequate meal in the middle of the day and another fairly early in the evening they do not suffer so much as the Duchess of Bedford did. If the Russian one meal a day accounted for so much tea-drinking in Russia it is at least possible that more regular meals in this country could contribute almost as much as the competition from other beverages to our decreased dependence on tea.

In these days when foods and drinks which we have relied on for years so often turn out to be killing us by degrees it might be as well to quote from the Tea Council's *Facts about Tea* what the medical authorities say about the effect of tea on the constitution.

'A cup of tea contains, on average, a little under a grain of caffeine and about two grains of tannin. When the infusion is drunk, the caffeine is released gradually and the tannin is allayed by the casein in the milk. The comforting effect of the warmth of the drink is at once felt, but the stimulus due to the caffeine comes about a quarter of an hour later.

'There is no evidence that tannin (or tannic acid) "tans the inside of your stomach", as if it were leather. The fact that tea stains the inside of pots and cups has nothing whatever to do with this.

'Tea chemists in fact seldom speak of "tannin" at all, but refer to "the polyphenols in tea". This is to distinguish them from "phenolic materials in tree-barks" which are apparently the "tannic acid" used for tanning leather.

'Tea is a true stimulant (unlike alcohol, which is really a depressant) because it contains caffeine (4% by weight in the leaf). It is thus the ideal reviver on a long car journey. Coffee contains 2% caffeine by weight in the leaf, and its stimulating effect is quicker than that of tea but it does not last so long.

'There is also no evidence that "tea is indigestible". For normally constituted people this cannot possibly be so unless the tea is made wrongly or "stewed' (e.g. the teapot is allowed to simmer on the hob, or new leaves are added to old leaves in the pot.)

'Tea is beneficial at all times of the day, but particularly on waking up and after meals. Together with the milk in it, it has a "buffering" action on the stomach acids which have been collecting during sleep. It takes the heaviness out of a meal by promoting peristalsis (getting the intestinal muscles moving). There are also certain enzymes in tea which promote digestion. Another effect of tea is to inhibit the action of the vagus nerve, which causes stomach glands to overproduce acid when one is anxious or excited. This is what we mean when we say that tea is both reviving *and* soothing. Recent American experiments have indicated that tea also protects the arteries from "freezing up".'

Tea is harmless, tea is even beneficial, tea is cheap. Every year we consume in Britain nearly 9 lb. per head of comforting, familiar tea, and although its popularity may rise and fall with the changing fashions, there must surely always be a place for it in every self-respecting British home.

II

Market Trends and New Developments

While the post-war years marked a falling off in the demand for tea, the late 1950's and the 1960's saw tremendous changes in the British coffee trade. Within this decade, sales of coffee doubled, and many factors combined to create a great revival in coffee-drinking.

First of all, the war left behind in England a considerable number of continental exiles who wanted to drink the kind of coffee they had enjoyed in their native lands. Apart from the popularity of coffee bars in the early 1950's the British public began to acquire more adventurous tastes with increasing foreign travel, and continental holidays introduced them to continental coffee, which was often not as good as the inexperienced tourists believed. The arrival of large numbers of American tourists added to the demand. Commercial television helped too. The bigger companies took advantage of the new medium by extensive advertising of instant coffee, all of which made the public more coffee-conscious.

Then British caterers, realizing they had to offer good coffee to overseas visitors, were helped by the enterprising new marketing policy of the coffee importers who packed ground coffee in vacuumized polythene pouches which were easier to store and to handle and much easier to use. Modern brewing equipment arrived to take the uncertainty out of coffee-making, ensuring perfect results every time, provided the equipment was used properly and the catering staff were competent.

Hoteliers and caterers found a new interest in coffee, and many began to study, usually for the first time in their lives, the different blends and qualities which were on the market. In addition to the range of pure blends, coffee with fig and coffee with chicory gained popularity. Fig and chicory were originally substances which were added to coffee to make it go further at times when coffee was either dear or scarce, but today they are more often used to give an interesting variation to the flavour. Fig roasted with coffee was a Turkish innovation which was taken up by the Viennese when they found that it was pleasant to drink and made a stronger liquor. Coffee with chicory is usually associated with France, where it was added to obtain the same effect. The standard of coffee served in British hotels and restaurants took a turn for the better.

For many years instant coffee (and at first instant tea also) was made by the 'spray-dried' method and increased sales of coffee were promoted by the fact that coffee from vending machines found readier acceptance than tea. There was no denying that in the early days vended tea did not measure up in quality and flavour to tea freshly made in a teapot.

Most important of all, coffee-drinking simply became fashionable again. Instead of having a cup of coffee just at mid-morning or after dinner in a restaurant, Englishmen began to enjoy coffee at all times of the day. Though coffee remained more expensive than tea, rising prosperity brought it within the reach of millions more people. By 1970 coffee was no longer strange, exotic and rather foreign. It had become part of Britain's everyday life.

Barbara Castle and her breathalyser hastened the trend by opening up a new market for coffee in the public houses. Licensees realized they would have to serve non-alcoholic drinks also to their motoring customers. Coffee was the answer, and a growing number of modern filter machines made their appearance behind the bar. Many licensees built up a thriving trade in coffee which they would never have dreamed of a year or two earlier.

Naturally, it is in the interests of the producing countries to promote the sale of coffee as much as they can, and in 1964 the International Coffee Council formed a World Coffee Promotion Committee which devotes about £2 million a year to coffee advertising. The scope for such advertising varies throughout the world. For instance China is not a coffee-drinking country and probably never will be, but at the other end of the scale Sweden already consumes nearly 30 lb. of green coffee per head so that advertising could hardly hope to achieve more. The largest potential market is still the North American countries and Europe. Here, coffee is established already, but there is room for increased consumption. The United States, the natural target for advertising because of its wealth, is not such a great coffee-drinking country as it used to be. While young people in this country are enthusiastically taking to coffee, the youth of America seems to be giving it up. This is dangerous for the future of coffee, and the World Promotion Committee are anxious in case coffee in America acquires the slightly 'elderly' image that tea was left with here. Most of the advertising has been directed at the young to convince them that coffee is a 'think drink' which will stimulate their brains when it most matters.

Britain, like other tea-drinking countries, is also promising ground for coffee promotion. Here the task is to persuade the public to stop drinking a cup of hot something and drink a hot cup of something else, and again the campaign is aimed at the young who will be tomorrow's heads of families and compilers of the grocery lists. In this country there is comparatively little advertising of ground coffee and a great deal of advertising of instant coffee of various kinds, but to the producing countries the benefit is the same.

Naturally, exports are vital to the developing countries, and most countries which produce coffee are poor and desperately need foreign exchange. Coffee is one of the most important commodities in the world. For instance it accounts for more than two-thirds of Colombia's export trade. Other Latin-American producing countries generally get about a third of their foreign income from coffee, while in Africa the proportion can be even higher. Coffee is measured in 60-kilo bags, and in the ten years from 1958 to 1968 the world export of coffee rose from about 36 million bags to 54 million bags, a record total. Of this total, Brazil, always thought of as the world's major coffee producer, accounted for only a third. Traditionally, South and Central America have always been concerned with grow- ing arabica coffee, the finer-flavoured coffee which fetches the highest price, but with the popularity of instant, soluble coffees, the African countries, which found the coarser robusta coffees more suitable to their climates, have been seizing a larger share of the market. Soluble coffees use a great deal of robustas in preference to arabicas, whose flavour would for the most part be lost. The United States, which consumes a great deal of instant coffee, has therefore been taking larger and larger proportions of robusta coffee from countries like Uganda and Angola which would not have found a market for their coffees before in an area which has hitherto been the preserve of arabicas.

However, with the recent advances in the technique of accelera- ted freeze drying, arabica coffees from South America have been in demand again in Europe for the manufacture of the newest soluble instant coffee.

A complicating factor in the world trade figures is the home consumption of coffee in the producing countries themselves, and the World Coffee Promotion Committee is encouraging this as being to the benefit of the coffee producers.

A coffee grower has always had a hazardous time. At worst his crop can be completely and permanently destroyed by disease, at best he faces the prospect of planting coffee which will not come into bearing for several years, not knowing whether there will be a market for the coffee when it is harvested. Before the war the burning of vast quantities of unsaleable Brazilian coffee hit the world's headlines. Even in 1969 Brazil held stocks of coffee equal to world consumption for one whole year. For the sake of the 20 million people who make their living by producing coffee as well as the many millions more who drink it, it was obviously desirable that production and consumption should be brought into some sort of balance, and in 1962 the International Coffee Organisation was set up in London by producing and consuming countries to try to stabilize the world coffee trade.

The most important of their achievements was the International Coffee Agreement which aims to settle a fair and equitable price for producers and consumers of coffee. The price was governed largely by the price that the United States consumers, as the largest market, were prepared to pay for their coffee, and since they are a wealthy country the price has probably seemed unreasonably high to the British housewife, particularly if she has read in the paper about the huge stocks of coffee in the world's warehouses. However, a complementary achievement of the International Coffee Agreement was to discourage the uncontrolled production of coffee by growers who might be misled by a freak rise in coffee prices.

All through the 1960's there were grumbles about the vast stocks of coffee and even the International Coffee Agreement machinery for dealing with depressed prices could no longer cope. Everyone had forgotten that tropical crops such as tea and coffee are always liable to sudden disaster, and the disaster is not always small and local, such as a flood, but large and devastating like the coffee blight which struck Ceylon in 1869 and cleared the island of coffee for good.

Costa Rica, a small Latin-American country growing a high-grade coffee, was badly affected only a few years ago when a volcanic eruption spread hot ash over a considerable area. But the worst danger of a more common sort is frost, and in July 1969 Brazil was hit by the worst frost in its coffee-growing history. Parana, the most important coffee-producing state, lost three-quarters of its crop overnight and half Brazil's total crop was lost. Still with pictures of overflowing warehouses in its mind, the coffee trade failed to take in the significance of the disaster, and the Coffee Council, still thinking in terms of glut, went ahead in August and fixed the world export quota at a very low level, expecting that they would have a difficult job keeping the price of coffee up unless they created an artificial shortage and filled the warehouses still fuller.

Gradually it dawned on everyone that there was a genuine shortage. Buyers began to compete for high-quality coffee and the price fixed under the Coffee Agreement was left way behind, overtaken by demand. If there had not been those notoriously large stocks piling up over the years, the coffee-drinkers of the world might have had a very nasty shock indeed. As the price of fine arabicas rose because of the shortage, they pulled the prices of robustas up with them, although the futures market in robustas kept their price more stable since a good deal of the crop was sold in advance of the news. One of the unfortunate effects of frost is that not only the crop but also the coffee plant is severely affected and new bushes have to be planted which take at least three or four years to come into bearing. Brazil foresaw that her coffee stocks would be exhausted by 1973, or even earlier if there were other setbacks, and she was naturally very concerned that other coffee-producing countries would steal her markets while she had not enough coffee to sell.

In the meantime, importers will have to make do with lower-quality coffee and increased prices for coffee generally. The International Coffee Organisation, on the other hand, has a chance to turn its attention from restrictive agreements to devising some positive action to guide its members towards a more mutually beneficial and rational policy. It will not have an easy task.

From the point of view of the producers, the International Coffee Agreement has been a good thing. It has not been easy to organize a marketing policy which would satisfy forty tropical producing countries, most of them very poor and desperately in need of exports, and also a great number of rich importing countries, all experienced in handling competitive markets. The most important participant by far has been the United States, and in fact it was on the insistence of the late President Kennedy that she did take part as a means of benefiting the alliance with Latin America.

At first the main aim of the agreement was to restrict the amount of coffee which came on to the world market in order to shore up the price and keep it stable, but then it started to make adjustments in the quotas of the various grades of coffee as they became scarcer or more plentiful. They in turn have independent controls which vary with the demand, and the information which the producing countries get from their association helps them to regulate the level of coffee production within their own countries. Brazil was the first country to discourage the uneconomic growing of coffee, and a fund was set up to help producers diversify out of coffee and also to support the World Coffee Promotion Council.

The other major steadying factor which influences coffee prices is the Coffee Terminal Market Association of London, which was established in 1958 to protect traders in coffee against adverse price fluctuations. This London terminal, as a futures market, is the only viable coffee terminal market in the world. With the success of this market London has become *the* market for trading in robusta coffee and a substantial proportion of the world robusta trade is now handled by London houses. One of the reasons for its success is that it operates on practical terms which are laid down by its Association with all contracts guaranteed by the London Produce Clearing House.

There are futures markets in other crops, cocoa is a good example, and they all work in a similar way. The success of the individual operators rests on their ability to interpret world conditions and anticipate supply and demand trends and act accordingly. To offset the risk inherent in fluctuating prices, merchants and dealers hedge on the London Terminal Market, which means their 'paper' transactions on the terminal market offset possible fluctuations in the physical market, or actual coffee beans.

Traders who wish to protect themselves against a fall in the price of coffee sell futures contracts. This is known as a 'selling hedge', while the buying of coffee futures as protection against a rise in price is known as a 'buying hedge'. Hedging is important, not only as a protection for the commercial interests dealing in coffee, but also to make financing the deals easier. The banks play a very big part in the commodity markets by advancing money against coffee offered as security. They naturally take a more favourable view of a contract if it is protected against a price change by a 'hedge'.

A contract unit on the London Terminal Market is five long tons, but there is no limit on the number of contract units which may be entered into at any one time. When the need for the 'hedge' ceases to exist, the terminal contract is offset by a reverse transaction. The number of contracts that are carried through to the date of maturity of the contract, and delivered as physical coffee, is usually less than 1%. This demonstrates that the London Terminal Market is mostly an insurance market, not a source of supply for coffee.

Trading is carried on at present at the London Commodity Exchange, Plantation House, although there are plans for new accommodation in 1972, and all trading is done by 'loud outcry' on the floor of the market. This ensures that it is a market *'ouvert'*. Prices are known immediately and as the various news agencies have representatives on the trading floor throughout trading hours the prices and trends can be transmitted throughout the world in a matter of minutes.

The Coffee Market Association of London consists of thirty-five floor members, which is the maximum permitted to trade on the floor of the market. Associate membership is unlimited and the number is continually expanding. While the International Coffee Agreement tends to govern the fluctuations normally caused by the laws of supply and demand, on occasions exceptional fluctuations in the price of any particular coffee is possible.

The futures transactions which take place on the coffee exchange only apply to the robusta coffee which comes mainly from Africa, but may eventually extend to arabicas and milds, traditionally sold by direct contract with the buyer. Brazils, which are under government control, would not be included. Such an expansion would add to the Coffee Terminal Market's contribution to Britain's invisible earnings and protect producers against the disadvantages of hurried sales.

Coffee still has a long way to go before it overtakes tea in popularity, but in 1970 the consumption of coffee in Britain reached the surprising figure of $3\frac{1}{2}$ lb. per head, while tea fell to $8\frac{1}{2}$ lb. per head, which was the lowest level since rationing was abolished. We still drink only a quarter as much coffee per head as people in America and on the Continent, and the Swedes consume a record $28\frac{1}{2}$ lb. each every year. The British are still not drinkers of ground coffee, since four-fifths of our coffee is processed into instant coffee, and, of the remaining fifth, a large proportion goes to restaurants and other catering organizations rather than into the shops for use in people's homes.

Although instant coffee is a great success story in itself, it had a slow start because of the war and it was not until some years later that Nescafé swept through the land to claim and hold the largest share of the instant-coffee market. Nescafe's biggest rival was Maxwell House, but in the past few years many other brands of instant coffee have come on the market, and—contrary to popular rumour which has been gaining ground recently—they are not 'all the same and only the label is different'. The blends of coffee and the strengths from which the spray-dried coffee is processed vary greatly, as greatly indeed as coffee at home may vary when it is made from different brands and qualities of ground coffee. What is true is that a very few manufacturers specialize in processing instant coffee by their plant, which is very complicated and expensive, and the coffee companies specify which blend and quality coffee they want processed. The price is generally a fair indication of the quality of instant coffee.

Spray-dried 'instant' immediately proved an acceptable substitute for ground coffee, which many housewives found daunting to make and rather expensive, and in the late 1960's it was joined by a new innovation, accelerated freeze-dried instant coffee which came in larger granules than spray-dried coffee and smelled and tasted a good deal more like 'real' coffee. Again Nescafé were first in the field with their Gold Blend and they mounted a massive advertising campaign to launch it, and again they were followed by Maxwell House. Manufacturers of accelerated freeze-dried coffee hope that the newer product will expand the total market for coffee and not merely transfer public preference from instant to newer instant.

Accelerated freeze drying is an expensive process. The capital cost of plant per unit of output is much higher than for spray drying, and the process includes low-temperature refrigeration and high-vacuum technology. The procedure for producing the liquor for accelerated freeze drying is similar to that used for spray drying except that the concentration is much higher and the liquor is foamed with gas to produce the correct bulk density in the finished product. This foaming process is usually carried out in a modified soft-ice-cream machine—a hoyer. The foam is then put into trays and passed into a cold room where it is frozen, broken, ground and sieved into particles of the desired size distribution. These particles are then transferred to trays which are loaded on to carriers and conveyed into a high-vacuum chamber where the trays are lowered on to heated plates. The dwell-time in this chamber is several hours and the combination of applied heat and high-vacuum conditions causes the ice to sublime in exactly the same way that a block of solid carbon dioxide vapourizes without melting, i.e. the coffee dries without passing through a liquid state. The carrier with the dried product then passes through an air lock where the product returns to normal condition of pressure and temperature.

More recently the new process of agglomeration has been applied to coffee and it has been introduced into the United Kingdom by General Foods who make Maxwell House instant coffee. In this process the standard spray-dried product is manufactured, ground and then partially re-wetted with steam and/or water in order to make the powder stick together to form large granules. Because it is an additional process after spray drying, the product is more expensive than spray-dried coffee, but appreciably cheaper than freeze-dried coffee, though there is no difference to the taste.

Accelerated freeze-dried tea is slightly different in that a tea concentrate has to be prepared first. With due regard to the disappointments of spray-dried tea, the first A.F.D. teas have proved most encouraging.

Our long habit of bracketing tea and coffee together makes them appear to have a similarity which in fact they do not have at all. Apart from the obvious fact that they both end up as hot drinks, they are as different as it is possible for two tropical crops to be. Coffee is a straightforward farmer's crop which does not need much expert knowledge to grow and with fruits which are harvested and marketed in much the same way as cocoa with only some basic processing to turn them into green-bean form before shipping. Farmers often produce coffee along with other crops and it can be grown quite successfully by African farmers with a little experience and guidance. Coffee growers usually finance themselves—that is they do not run plantations which are owned by limited companies.

Tea, on the other hand, is an industry which not only grows the plant but turns the plucked leaves into chests of finished tea on the estates, and the plantations and their factories must be efficiently run. Apart from tea in China, the tea industry has largely been financed by British capital ever since 1834. The investments for the most part paid off handsomely, but it was necessary to provide the finance from Britain in this way because tea is one of the most expensive crops in the world. Not only is there the considerable cost of clearing jungle and terracing, but a factory has to be built and equipped, and tea under cultivation requires a very large labour force, in the case of some of the larger Ceylon and African plantations running into several thousands.

As the tea industry became highly organized, agency houses in India and Ceylon grew up to handle the affairs of the plantations on behalf of the owning companies, which, of course, were in London. Most of the agency houses had holdings in the plantations with which they were concerned and they kept the remote estates in touch with the demands of the world tea market. There were occasional slumps resulting from over-production, but in general the tea companies made high profits, much of which were spent on improved cultivation, irrigation, terracing and fertilizers.

With independence, trouble came from the new governments which saw the tea industry as a lucrative source of revenue. There were, of course, many Indian and Sinhalese plantation owners who had been rich landowners and seen the potential of growing tea themselves, but the British plantations still had a virtual monopoly of the best tea fetching the highest prices.

It was in Ceylon that the first intimations of real trouble came. There were riots and acts of terrorism on the plantations and the threat of nationalisation. Some clergymen's widows realised with a shock that the 40% they had come to expect on their Ceylon tea shares was not as safe as they had imagined. Then the trouble subsided. There was certainly a drop in share prices and a gradual natural change-over from British ownership of estates to Sinhalese ownership, but no state appropriation. Ceylon had not got the money to pay compensation to the tune of millions of pounds to the owning companies and could not risk a hostile reaction from the country which was her largest market. On the contrary, she needed foreign capital investment in Ceylon, and British money in the tea estates was part of this. British tea companies could not sell their estates and take their money out of Ceylon, but for a long time they could sell and transfer the money from one estate to another or open up new estates.

By 1969, when Ceylon celebrated the centenary of the founding of her tea industry, the depressed world market in tea had replaced nationalisation as the main cause for concern. As long as tea companies are having a hard struggle to maintain profitability, the temptation to nationalize is likely to be weaker, but it is a skeleton which is still taken out of its cupboard and rattled from time to time, particularly when the government in power is in favour of radical change.

The Indian Government also found the tea industry a valuable source of revenue and went further than Ceylon in imposing taxes. There were both export and excise duties and all sorts of other local taxes such as the Assam carriage tax and the West Bengal entry tax which whittled away a good deal of income at a time when the producing companies had other expenses to consider. The workers on the estates demanded more money. A rise in wages for a very large labour force is a serious thing. Tea is sold on the open market for what it will fetch in the auctions of London and Calcutta. If costs rise, there is no way of passing them on to the customer and the price of Indian tea all through the 1960's was falling rather than rising.

For some of the plantations producing medium- and lower-priced teas, the situation reached a stage where they were no longer profitable. They were badly hit by the newer teas from Africa, which were improving all the time and had the advantage of government encouragement. In 1959 India supplied nearly half of Britain's tea; ten years later the proportion was down to a quarter. In 1969 it was reported that at the prices then ruling in London, many Indian tea producers were selling at a loss. During the ten years up to 1969 the value of Indian tea shares dropped by half.

In 1969 at the height of the plucking season about 200,000 workers on the plantations in north-east India struck for seventeen days. This strike cost the industry more than £30 million in lost production and during this crucial time the tea bushes were neglected and allowed to become wild and out of control, with poor-quality leaf. The Dooars district was particularly hard-hit. Economic prospects looked for a time so bleak that more excitable commentators in Calcutta foresaw the ruin of the Indian tea industry. The British buyers were blamed for not paying more for the tea, and the British consumer was blamed for not drinking more of it. The *bara sahib* up in the manager's bungalow was blamed for his old-fashioned production methods which aimed to produce good, orthodox tea, or alternatively he was criticized for his modern methods which sacrificed quality to quantity and appearance of liquor. Production companies blamed competition from Africa and increased labour costs. Everybody blamed the Indian Government and its heavy taxation. The Government decided to abolish the export tax and increase and redistribute the excise duties. This pleased nobody, particularly the Assam and Darjeeling growers whose shares of the excise duty were approximately doubled and trebled respectively.

Darjeeling is well known for the high prices which some of its teas fetch in the auctions, £3·75 per pound is not uncommon, but the bulk of Darjeeling tea does not come into this class, the yield per acre is low and production costs are high and the need for modernisation is urgent. Many of the tea bushes are ninety years old and even with a modest replacement rate of 1½% a year, some will be 150 years old before they are uprooted.

Harassed both by high excise duties and the Bengal entry tax which had to be paid on all tea going to Calcutta to be auctioned and shipped, the Assam provincial government decided to open its own tea auction centre at Gauhati and arrange for the tea bought by foreign buyers to be transported 1,100 miles or so across India to the port of Kandla 200 miles eastward along the coast from Karachi on the Arabian Sea. This plan, received with reservations in some quarters, was first put into operation in September 1970, and although it is only to be expected that a period of teething troubles will occur, some alternative to congested Calcutta and its strike-prone docks may well prove a healthy development.

Meanwhile, the Indian and Ceylon tea industries digested the facts with which they had to come to terms. The first was that their internal tax troubles had no bearing on prevailing world prices and

The tea auction room in Sir John Lyon House, the new centre of the London tea trade. Photograph taken on opening day.

Coffee Terminal Market, Plantation House, Mincing Lane, London. Bids are made by 'loud outcry' on the floor of the house.

Drying tower used in the manufacture of instant coffee by the spray drying process.

Extractors for making instant coffee.

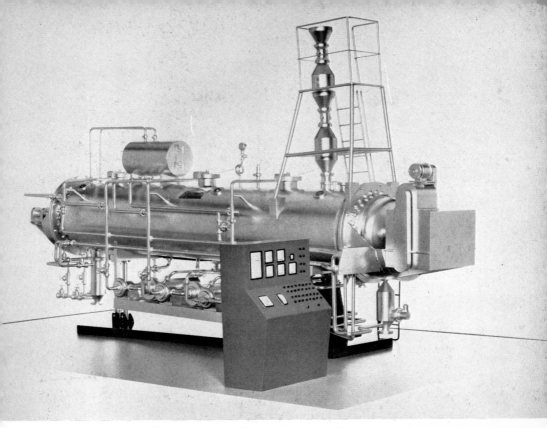

Continuous coffee extractor for making coffee liquor for use in instant or freeze-dried coffee.

Mombasa charity tea auction held during the 1971 Tea Convention
Mr. D. G. Davies, Managing Director of Africa Tea Brokers Ltd.
is presenting a cheque from the proceeds to President Kenyatta's
private secretary.

the second was that world consumption would not automatically rise to match increased world production.

These problems were endemic and had been for many years, but they have intensified since the rise of the East and Central African countries, particularly Kenya, to compete in the same export markets. They were problems which the individual countries could not hope to overcome themselves and during the late 1960's the first moves were made by the Consultative Committee on Tea set up by the Food and Agriculture Organisation of the United Nations to negotiate an export quota system. An agreement of this sort had been tried before, notably in 1933 when the tea-exporting world was mostly India, Ceylon and the Dutch East Indies. It was found then that although delicate to negotiate, a quota system was not impossible to operate. Since then the situation has become more complicated. India and Ceylon, who have lived with the problem of low prices for years, were in favour, in principle, of a quota system, but the question was whether the African countries, whose teas were improving and who were committed to heavy expansion programmes, would be prepared to co-operate. A bridging agreement kept 90 million pounds of tea off the export markets during 1970 and had a beneficial effect on the prices of tea in the international auctions. Late in 1970 forty tea-exporting and -importing nations took part in a conference in New Delhi which was a hopeful indication that by the target of 1972 real progress will have been made towards controlling, if not completely solving, the difficulties of the tea industry.

The internal consumption of the producing countries plays a large part in the health of their tea industries. Ceylon consumes a good deal of the tea she grows, and India's domestic consumption is rising steadily. This protects growers with low profitability who would prefer to supply a steady home market rather than risk the vagaries of the international market. Pakistan, whose tea-growing area in Bengal almost exclusively turns out medium-quality tea, has ceased to export and is now consuming the whole of her tea output herself, and even importing a little. China is the supreme example of a major tea-producing country which can absorb all its production. A sufficiently large home consumption transfers the problem of international tea prices from the tea producer to the government of the country which has to decide what importance to put on its export trade and adjust its taxation to favour exporters if necessary.

Ceylon has always given her tea industry high priority, as it makes up the major part of her trade. Her acreage under tea has increased and her exports to Britain are half as much again as they

L

were in 1953, a marked contrast to India's decline. She has also realized the value of advertising and the standard of her public relations in the tea-importing countries is very impressive.

Next to Asia, the most important continent where tea is grown is Africa. British producing companies opened up the tea-growing areas of Africa in much the same way as they did in India, but with the benefit of their earlier years of experience. At first, as with Indian tea, they had to start with an inferior quality and improve it by patient cultivation, and because the production costs were low they could afford to accept low prices in the London auction in the early years until improved quality won greater acceptance from the buyers and created a demand.

Kenya has two features which make the country particularly suited to growing good tea—altitude and rainfall. The principal tea-growing districts are the Kenya Highlands, an extensive area lying between Mount Kenya and Lake Victoria on either side of the Rift Valley. These highlands range in altitude from 5,000 to 9,000 feet and because plucking is possible for most of the year, the financial return on plantations is very high, an important consideration now that the capital cost of a tea plantation, including a factory, is estimated to be at least £500 an acre.

Commercial tea companies have poured finance into the Kenya tea industry and there has been tremendous concentration on breeding higher-yielding tea plants producing improved-quality tea. On the manufacturing side, the new plantations have the most advanced equipment in the world with Rotorvanes, developed at the Tocklai experimental station in North India as recently as 1958, being used almost universally to produce both orthodox and C.T.C. (Crush, Tear and Curl) teas, replacing the older conventional batch rollers. These newer methods have cut down the labour necessary in the factory, although the tea industry generally is one of the largest employers of labour in Kenya.

Side by side with tea production by commercial companies is a scheme for smallholders which was started in the 1950's and is now run by the Kenya Tea Development Authority, which is self-financing. Similar schemes are now working in most other African territories with suitable climates, notably Uganda.

These African producing countries are more dependent on their exports than the older Asian producers since their internal tea consumption at present is negligible. Also they are financed by new, expensive money, while Indian and Ceylon plantations redeemed their original investments many years ago when dividends were high. The companies investing in African tea plantations cannot hope to look forward to a century operating practically free from government interference and high taxation, and although they have enjoyed a period when they have been lightly taxed by the African Exchequers, the benevolence of governments is as little to be relied on as the favour of kings, and the President of Kenya is already expecting the tea industry to increase its labour force to relieve unemployment.

Political affiliations have their effect on the international tea market as they do on other forms of trade. Until 1966 Russia imported a good deal of tea from China, but since their ideological disagreement there has been no trade. Ever since 1957 Russia has expanded her tea production in the Caucasus to such a spectacular extent that she may soon be able to supply all the tea she requires. Since the Russian tea estates are the most northerly in the world, about the same latitude as the north of Italy, the small-leaved China variety is grown. At present Russia is a keen buyer of the best-quality Indian teas, and takes the bulk of the Darjeeling and good Assam at high prices, bidding British buyers out of the market. Even when Russian tea production is sufficient for imported tea to be unnecessary, it is likely that Russia buyers will still be powerful in the Calcutta and Gauhati auctions simply because they like the tea.

Indonesia, one of the oldest black-tea producers, naturally has strong ties with the Netherlands, whose colony she once was. A lot of the Indonesian tea used by British blenders comes through the Dutch tea exchange which is the oldest in Europe. In 1959 trading in Amsterdam was discontinued and the centre for the Netherlands tea trade is now Antwerp.

Green teas are still made in Formosa and Japan. A good deal of this goes to the United States, but the other big consumer is Morocco. Japan once exported 10 million pounds of tea a year to Morocco, but now this market has been taken by China and, apart from her trade with the United States, Japan has ceased to be an exporting country.

The newest continent to start producing exportable tea is South America. For many years the tea grown on that continent was of no commercial importance. Now there is a rapidly expanding tea-growing area in the Argentine, together with a few thousand acres in Brazil which were pioneered by Japanese immigrants at the turn of the century. Neither Brazil nor the Argentine is a tea-drinking country, Brazil naturally preferring coffee, in any case, but they do have on their doorstep a very convenient market in Chile, which alone among the South American nations drinks nearly as much per head as Canada.

There are many lesser tea-producing countries, but they are all sensitive to the weakness or strength of the demand in London.

Their tea is for the most part quite useful, but not vital to the big blending companies, and an international crisis, such as Suez in 1956, can distort the market to such an extent that a small country can find itself a big exporter one year and hardly able to sell any tea the next. Iran's exports in 1957 were 18 million pounds but the following year this had fallen to half a million. There is also the understandable reluctance of buyers to become dependent on tea from countries which are known to be prone to earthquakes, floods and general disasters. Some countries have a climate which barely supports tea, Russia and the Middle East are notable examples, and a slight variation in rainfall or temperature is far more serious there than in traditional tea climates. This is an unhappy situation for the growers, but buyers are rarely affected since tea is now grown over such widely diffused areas of the world that a drought in one place is usually balanced by an unexpectedly good crop somewhere else.

A significant new arrival is South Africa which now has plantations with tea in production. South Africa has always been an important customer for Ceylon tea, and although the new industry is in its infancy, Ceylon must view it with apprehension. There is also a tiny tea industry in Queensland, Australia, but this is not likely to become extensive because the cost of a labour force large enough to keep a modern tea plantation in production would be astronomical. Only the most extreme degree of mechanization could make Australian tea worth developing.

No section of the tea industry can exist in isolation, and British consumption, which can account for 50% or more of the tea exports of a producing country, is a powerful factor. To understand how the situation abroad is to some extent influenced by the British quarter-pound packet trade it is necessary to trace the quite radical developments which have taken place during the past twenty years.

When tea was de-rationed in 1953 it was the first time there had been a free market for fourteen years. The critical capacity of the public had almost disappeared, and after the dramatic fall in tea prices on Wild Wednesday in 1955 and the introduction by the big blenders of cheap blends, the pattern was set which has never altered since. The public has bought tea on price. During the 1950's the new C.T.C. (Crush, Tear and Curl) manufactured teas came on the market in larger quantities. They produced a bright, coloury liquor which infused quickly and although some buyers who liked the appearance of the tea deplored the effect of such methods of manufacture on the quality, the public were perfectly willing to accept the time-saving factor of quick-brewing teas as the superior benefit.

The spread of instant coffee encouraged the trend. When the super-markets opened in greater and greater numbers and slashed the price of tea as a 'loss leader' to the point where their own profit was negligible, the public accepted this too and became accustomed to buying its tea at a price which in the long run was to do no good to anybody.

All through the sixties costs rose. The costs of storage and distri-bution rose in the blending companies too, but they managed to absorb them. The public did not seem to want orthodox Indian teas with fine flavour, so the buyers bought them the new African teas which had the necessary leaf size, bright appearance and quick infusion and at first were cheaper. The competition for the quarter-pound packet trade was keen and the few large companies which supplied it dared not raise their prices singly and risk losing their market.

By 1970 the price of tea had remained stable for thirteen years, but the Indian and Ceylon growers of good, orthodox teas were in dire straits. The chairman of a Ceylon producing company told his shareholders that his company and others had seen their tea sold in the Colombo and London auctions in 1969 at the lowest price for eighteen years. For many North Indian gardens actual ruin was not far off. There was certainly a buyer's market, but there were no new tea companies competing for the British retail market. The membership of the Tea Buyers Association declined from 113 in 1956 to forty-one in 1970. During the same period some of the famous names in tea ceased to be independent companies. Brooke Bond merged with Leibig Extract of Malt Co. Ltd. to become Brooke Bond Oxo. Typhoo was bought by Cadbury-Schweppes. Twinings, a relatively small company concentrating on the market for more expensive 'speciality' blends, became part of Garfield Weston's biscuit empire. Lyons and the Co-operative Wholesale Society were always well diversified, although the C.W.S. had been having its period of difficulties. These companies, between them, accounted for 90% of the retail trade in the United Kingdom.

In Mincing Lane the brokers also suffered from the stagnation and the increasing tendency to sell teas in local auctions in Calcutta, Colombo and Nairobi rather than London. Darjeeling tea no longer came to London to be sold. The Tea Brokers' Association, consisting of five brokerage firms where there had been nineteen in 1956, economised by ceasing to put out its catalogues for the weekly auctions to be printed and started to print them itself, at a saving of several thousand pounds a year. The association members, living on their fixed incomes, which were the result of earning the same commission on teas which had not risen in price in fifteen years, reached the point where they could no longer afford the steeply rising rents on their offices in Plantation House. A syndicate of twenty tea-broking, blending and merchanting tea firms bought the lease of accommodation at Sir John Lyon House in Upper Thames Street, and at the end of 1970 they moved. The auction room moved too, although the new smaller tea auditorium in Plantation House had only been in use for two years. The tea trade, which had been in Mincing Lane since before the days of the clipper races, was to be in the Lane no longer.

In the middle of 1970 Brooke Bond, supplier of 43% of the British market, and backed by Typhoo, J. Lyons and the other major blending companies, decided that they were not prepared to sacrifice the quality of their tea or contribute any more to the squeeze on tea growers. They raised the price of their popular quarter-pound packets. Immediately the price rise went to the Prices and Incomes Board, an organization which was disbanded soon afterwards. The Board severely criticized Brooke Bond as the prime mover in the general price rise and their report stunned the whole of the tea trade, both in the United Kingdom and abroad, by its complete failure to grasp the real issues involved. The Board attached little importance to the rise in handling and distribution costs which the tea companies, in common with other commercial firms, had had to bear during the past thirteen years. Instead they concentrated on the price of tea in the auctions which had generally fallen since 1959, not realizing that the prepressed prices were the result not only of over-production but also of the restriction in buying power of the big companies caused by the retail prices being too low. The tea trade does not start at the London Docks, but is part of a whole industry involving British planters, finance and shareholders and it was manifestly unreasonable that one section of the trade should be expected to keep down prices at the cost of running the other half out of business, which would certainly happen if buying price limits were set lower and lower.

Brooke Bond were surprised and dismayed at the reception their price rise was having but they were supported immediately and warmly by the tea industry in Britain and the producing countries. At last tea prices were to be allied to the realities of production and distribution. For the sake of the future quality of tea as well as common justice to the millions whose livelihood depends on it and the people who have financed it, the British public had to start paying a fair price for its tea. When an international quota system is operating, resulting from the negotiations of the Food and Agriculture Organisation, the effect and indeed the explicit intention, will be to hold prices of tea on the tea exchange at a level which is economic to the producers but not unfair to the consumers. This will mean more rises in tea prices as the developing countries raise their standard of living.

If the price rises make the public think harder about the quality of the tea they are drinking, this will be all to the good. People who wonder what has happened to the flavour in tea over the years should pause before they reach out for their usual packet of cheap tea and try instead one which is more expensive. All the blending companies produce excellent blends of quality teas which are always available and deserve to be far more widely appreciated. A few pence more give the buyer and blender spending power to buy good teas which transform a blend into something to be drunk with satisfaction. There is no reason why reviving quality should mean any loss of the convenience we are becoming used to. There is no suggestion that we should go back to those big tea leaves now that we are used to fannings. Tea bags, which already make up 10% of the retail market and are gaining popularity all the time, can, and often do, contain dust grades of leaf from good-quality tea which can be blended to give predominantly Indian or Ceylon flavours.

There remains instant tea, which is already in use in vending machines but as yet it is only maintaining a mere foothold in conventional markets. In the producing countries, where it is regarded both as a boon and as a threat, it has caused much agitation. Some see it as a blow to high-quality tea, which might not prove suitable for processing, but others envisage the manufacture of instant tea as a supplementary industry which could be carried on near the estates. In countries not used to leaf tea as we are in Britain, instant tea has great potential. In any event, it is likely to be several years before instant tea makes up a significant part of the British market.

Coffee- and tea-producing countries need their exports to survive and understandably they all show a tendency to over-produce. Since tea and coffee both employ a large amount of labour, this means that the standard of living of these countries depends on the consuming countries' ability to consume more and pay more for it. The two international organizations which have been formed to regulate the market as much as they can have a difficult task to reconcile the interests of both sides. In the same way that President Kennedy felt that the United States had a special responsibility to the coffee producers because of her vast buying power, so Britain has a special role to play in the tea agreement, not only as the largest consumer but because of her presence and experience over more than a century through the companies growing the tea. The fact that Britain has large investments in almost all the major tea-growing countries—and some producing companies have estates in both Africa and Asia—should prove a stabilizing and binding influence in a situation where nationalism could create the largest obstacle.

Although they have absorbed great changes in their 300-year history, the tea and coffee markets of London have usually presented a serene face to the world. To many they seem a quiet and prosperous section of the City, slightly old-fashioned, with perhaps a touch of oriental mystery and romance. To us who earn our living from tea and coffee this is an attractive picture too, and we look forward to the day when a prosperous serenity can be a reality. It will not be yet.

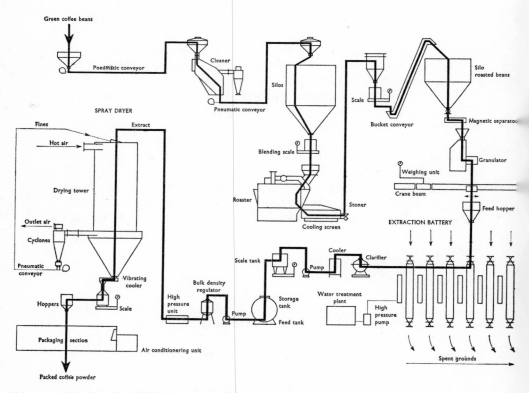

Diagram showing the NIRO instant-coffee-making process

Bibliography

Antrobus, H. A., *A History of the Assam Company* (Edinburgh: T. & A. Constable, 1957)

Huxley, Gervas, *Talking of Tea* (London: Thames & Hudson, 1956)

Harler, C. R., *The Culture and Marketing of Tea* (London: Oxford University Press, 1956)

Haarer, A. E., *Modern Coffee Production* (London: Leonard Hill (Books) Ltd., 1958)

Hainsworth, Ernest, *Tea Pests and Diseases and Their Control* (Cambridge: W. Heffer & Sons Ltd., 1952)

Johnson, Reginald J., *Johnson's Note Book for Tea Planters* (Alleppey, South India: The Santa Cruz Press, 1951)

Ellis, Aytoun, *The Perry Universities. A History of the Coffee Houses* (London: Secker & Warburg, 1956)

Farson, Negley, *Last Chance in Africa* (London: Victor Gollancz Ltd., 1949)

Van der Post, Laurence, *Venture to the Interior* (London: Hogarth Press, 1952)

Dundas, Sir Charles, *African Crossroads* (London: Macmillan & Co. Ltd., 1955)

Eden, T., *Tea* (Longmans, Green & Co. Ltd., 1958)

Wilson, Smithett & Co., *Tea Production in Africa, New Guinea and Australia* (1969)

Periodicals

International Vending Times (Published by Weald of Kent Publications Ltd.)

Investors Guardian Incorporating the Tea and Rubber Mail

International Tea Committee: Annual Bulletin of Statistics

Index

English boil

Filtering

Percolator

Vienna Incomparable

French drip

Early sypho

Le Brun's Cafetière

CONA

CONA

1920 Vacuum

Etiuscan biggin

Brain's pneumatic

Syphon